CW01271611

IMAGINATION IN THE CLASSROOM

Imagination in the Classroom

*Teaching and Learning
Creative Writing in Ireland*

Anne Fogarty, Éilís Ní Dhuibhne & Eibhear Walshe
EDITORS

FOUR COURTS PRESS

Set in 10.5 on 14 point Garamond for
FOUR COURTS PRESS LTD
7 Malpas Street, Dublin 8, Ireland
e-mail: info@fourcourtspress.ie
www.fourcourtspress.ie
and in North America for
FOUR COURTS PRESS
c/o ISBS, 920 N.E. 58th Street, Suite 300, Portland, OR 97213.

© The various contributors and Four Courts Press 2013

A catalogue record for this title
is available from the British Library.

ISBN 978-1-84682-413-5

All rights reserved. No part of this publication may be
reproduced, stored in or introduced into a retrieval system,
or transmitted, in any form or by any means (electronic,
mechanical, photocopying, recording or otherwise), without
the prior written permission of both the copyright owner
and the publisher of this book.

Printed and bound by CPI Group (UK) Ltd, Croydon, CR0 4YY

Contents

Acknowledgments	7
Introduction *Éilís Ní Dhuibhne with Anne Fogarty*	9
The history and practice of the teaching of creative writing in Ireland *Gerald Dawe*	24
Write first, worry later: fostering creativity in the classroom *Roddy Doyle*	35
On theft: teaching poetry composition to undergraduates *Sinéad Morrissey*	45
Beginnings: becoming a teacher of creative writing *Leanne O'Sullivan*	55
Imaginative constellations: the creative writing workshop as laboratory *Paul Perry*	63
'The helmet that never was': reflections on fiction and life writing *Carlo Gébler*	71
Virtual worlds: teaching creative writing in an online environment *Nessa O'Mahony*	81
'The Man in the Moon's autobiography': memoir and the creative writing workshop *Eibhear Walshe*	93

Ars longa, vita brevis: the novel, the workshop and time 101
Éilís Ní Dhuibhne

Writing as process: truth and sincerity in the poetry workshop 116
Mary O'Donnell

What we talk about when we talk about talking: writing
dialogue in the novel and short story 126
James Ryan

Grading creativity 136
Mary Morrissy

Contributors 142

Index 145

Acknowledgments

The editors would like to acknowledge financial assistance provided by the National University of Ireland Grant towards Scholarly Publication, the School of English Publication Fund, University College Cork, and the College of Arts, Celtic Studies and Social Sciences Publication Fund, University College Cork. We would like to thank Four Courts Press, the contributors and the Royal Irish Academy Committee for Literatures in English, especially Rebecca Farrell and Vanessa Carswell. Our thanks too to Fidelma Slattery for the cover design, and to Paul Farley and Michael Longley for permission to quote from their work.

Introduction

ÉILÍS NÍ DHUIBHNE

> At one time I thought the most important thing was talent. I think now that … the young man or the young woman must possess or teach himself, train himself, in infinite patience, which is to try and to try and to try until it comes right. He must train himself in ruthless intolerance.[1]

Opinion on the value of Creative Writing courses may still be divided, and the suspicion that it cannot be taught lingers. But it is hard to argue with William Faulkner's view cited above that great writing is the result of hard work, not, or not mainly, of the flash of inspiration – although there are exceptions to the general rule. From accepting that the young man or woman must teach or train himself or herself to write, it is a short step to acknowledging that the aspiring writer possessed of some essential aptitudes and skills (including literacy, verbal imagination and intelligence) can indeed benefit and learn from the experience of others, just as those embarking on careers as carpenters or physicians or engineers, not to mention musicians, visual artists, architects or dancers, in general spend many years learning their trades, with guidance from those who have practised it.

As Gerald Dawe, among those who may be credited with introducing Creative Writing as a degree subject to the Irish academy, points out in the opening essay in this collection, in which he offers an invaluable insider's overview of the history of the teaching of Creative Writing in Ireland, it is not a new discipline. It has had a formal academic footing in the US since 1936, when the Iowa Writers' Workshop, the first MFA programme in Creative Writing, was established, under the directorship of Wilbur Scham (to be succeeded by the more well-known Paul Engle). The Iowa Writers' Workshop, among whose alumni are numbered a host of the most prominent American writers, including Flannery O'Connor, Raymond Carver and Jane

---

1 William Faulkner, press conference, University of Virginia, 20 May 1957. See http://www.faulkner.lib.virginia.edu, accessed 12 January 2013.

Smiley, is generally regarded as the first academic degree course in Creative Writing in the world. Today, hundreds of north American universities, and many in the UK and Australia, offer undergraduate and graduate progammes in Creative Writing. So far largely confined to the Anglophone world, the subject is beginning to find a place in continental universities. The University of Stockholm, for instance, will begin an MA programme in September 2015 (under the auspices of the Department of English, however).

Ireland has only recently adopted Creative Writing as an academic discipline, in most instances somewhat tentatively, as a Masters programme rather than a core undergraduate subject. Anecdotal evidence suggests that attempts were made to introduce it in the 1970s,[2] and unaccredited workshops have been offered in some universities, such as University College Dublin, for decades.[3] But as Gerald Dawe recounts, Trinity College Dublin was the first university on the island of Ireland to offer a degree, an MPhil in Creative Writing, in 1998. This highly successful and much sought after programme broke the academic ice – and ice is the *mot propre*, if folklore is to be believed – and paved the way for the by now ubiquitous programmes. In 2002, an MA in Writing was offered for the first time in NUI Galway, under the direction of Adrian Frazier, and thanks to the efforts of Thomas Kilroy.[4] In 2006, Andrew Carpenter established an MA in Creative Writing in University College Dublin. Queen's University Belfast set up an MA in 1998, and a PhD in 2006.[5] Since 2008, NUI Maynooth has offered Creative Writing as part of its denominated entry BA programme in English[6] and University College Cork introduced an MA in Creative Writing in 2013.

The model of teaching Creative Writing in the Irish universities has naturally been influenced by the American prototype, particularly in the emphasis on the centrality of the workshop, but, as Gerald Dawe reminds us, Creative Writing workshops had dominated the scene from the 1960s onwards and consequently Irish universities were

[2] Personal communication with Maurice Harmon, professor emeritus of Anglo-Irish literature and drama at UCD.   [3] Creative writing workshops, although not included on the official curriculum, have been offered to UCD students in the Department of English since the late 1980s.   [4] Communication with Dr John Kenny, NUI Galway.   [5] Communication with Dr Sinead Morrissey, Queen's University Belfast.   [6] Communication with Professor Chris Morash, NUI Maynooth. Creative Writing was introduced when the English syllabus in Maynooth was completly re-organized, in 2008.

merely catching up with standard practice. As predecessors to current programmes, Dawe mentions 'The Group', writers who met under moderator Philip Hobsbaum in 1960s Belfast, and the National Writers' Workshop – a ten-week writers' course held in University College Galway in 1976, which continued as an annual event for several years; as well as Poetry Ireland workshops.

It is not easy to trace the rich history of Creative Writing workshops in Ireland, outside the academic context, and it is beyond the scope of this introduction to undertake this fascinating task in any detail. As Dawe indicates, the early 1970s appears to be the real starting point. Formations such as 'The Group' in Belfast had perhaps more in common with the kind of informal gatherings of writers to which the young W.B. Yeats, for instance, belonged, which met weekly in Katherine Tynan's farmhouse in County Dublin in 1885,[7] or the Rhymers' Club, which convened in the Cheshire Cheese pub in London in the 1890s.[8] Another example of a writers' group which was an indisputable precursor of those which flourish today – many of them run by and for women – was the Irish Women Writers' Club, founded in 1933 by Dorothy Macardle and Blanaid Salkeld. It survived for decades, and included among its members Rosamond Jacob, Hanna Sheehy Skeffington, Patricia Lynch and Theresa Deevy.[9] The Creative Writing workshop, course or university programme, has its local antecedents in such constellations of writers, who have for centuries felt the need to form circles where work is reviewed and writers learn from and encourage one another. According to R.F. Foster, contemporaries outside the Rhymers' Club 'saw it as an efficient machine for mutual admiration',[10] a description which many might regard as fitting for today's workshops also. Although the romantic perception of the writer as a lonely artist working alone on the edges of society is not without foundation – writing is almost always a solitary act in the first instance, even when group thinking is intrinsically involved at some levels[11] – the long history of formal and informal writers' groups indicates that co-existing with the desire for solitude is a frequent requirement of peer support, affirmation and shared insight or knowledge. The

7 R.F. Foster, *W.B. Yeats, a life: the apprentice mage, 1865–1914*. Volume 1 (Oxford, 1997), p. 55.   8 Ibid., p. 107.   9 Leeann Lane, *Rosamond Jacob: third person singular* (Dublin, 2010), p. 21.   10 Foster, *W.B. Yeats, a life*, p. 108.   11 This is the case in the creation of television drama serials, for instance.

Yeats who sincerely hankered after a Thoreau-like life among the beanrows on a lonely island was also a man who lived in cities and all his life belonged to literary societies that could well be described as writers' groups.

The key decade for the institution of the formal Creative Writing workshop in Ireland is the 1970s, with 1971 marking a particularly significant milestone. In June of that year, the first Listowel Writers' Week, the brainchild of Seamus Wilmot, Bryan MacMahon and John B. Keane, took place in the small north Kerry town. Listowel Writers' Week was the pioneer of the literary festival, now such a widespread and accepted feature of Irish cultural life. In 1972, three workshops were added to the Listowel programme of launches, readings, exhibitions and perfomances. Bryan McMahon conducted all three himself![12] It is possible that these were the first relatively formal Creative Writing workshops to be held in Ireland, although Irish writers such as Frank O'Connor, Sean Ó Faoláin, Mary Lavin, Benedict Kiely and others had taught courses in the area in American universities throughout the previous decades. Following their introduction to Listowel in 1972, the workshops became a core part of that particular festival.[13] Quite quickly, the concept of the writers' workshop gained in popularity, and by the end of the 1970s it was part of the Irish literary landscape – although not as prominent as it later became. Mary Morrissy, for instance, writes in this book that she attended only one writers' workshop in her life, since 'they were not part of the culture of 70s Ireland', indicating that some young writers were unaware of the phenomenon, a situation which would hardly be possible today.[14]

---

12 In an email communication Eilish Wren describes the history of the Listowel Writers' Week as follows: The first Writers' Week Festival took place from 2–6 June 1971. Seamus Wilmot, Registrar of the National University of Ireland, President of Writers' Week, and a native of Listowel, officially opened the festival. It was done by hoisting the flag of the Fitzmaurice family over Listowel Castle for the first time since 1600. There was quite a big group at the first meeting in 1970 when they started planning for the festival in 1971. Twenty to thirty members signed up as volunteers, but ... Seamus Wilmot, Bryan MacMahon and John B. Keane were the main people. The programme does not show any workshops taking place in 1971 contrary to what it says in our history document. It appears that Bryan MacMahon went to the States in 1971 and discovered the workshop concept. He actually directed the three workshops himself in 1972: 'The why of writing', 'The how of writing' and 'It is solved by writing'.   13 I participated in a workshop on the short story, faciliated by Emma Cooke, in 1978, at which time the concept of the workshop seemed to be firmly established in Listowel. It was the first creative writing workshop I encountered. 14 See below p. 36.

Although real life does not arrange itself neatly in decades for the convenience of historians, it is hardly accidental that the creative writing movement, if such it may be called and whatever its original seeds, found a firm foothold in Ireland in the 70s. The decade was a period of enormous transition in Ireland.[15] Old moulds were broken – political, social, educational, sexual and artistic. The democratization of education, following the introduction of free second-level education in 1966[16] and of university grants in 1971,[17] the growth of a vigorous and demanding feminism and the re-evaluation of outmoded sexual mores, created a society in which people, in greater numbers than ever before, had the urge and freedom to express themselves in many art forms. A loosening of the ideological stranglehold of conservative forces, religious and social, permitted an intellectual expansion, an opening of minds and imagination. People – especially those in oppressed or to some extent silenced groups, including gays, women and youth – could question the rigid values of the past, with some impunity. The atmosphere of the period encouraged such expression by those who in previous generations would have been denied access to official forms of literary creativity – such as the theatre, the novel or the poem – due to lack of education, money and social or legal status. New voices were not just tolerated, but welcomed, and there was plenty to write about, and against: anger and dissent are potent forces of inspiration, and the 1970s was both a liberating and a revolutionary decade in Ireland.

Moreover, in the context of the creative verbal imagination, the transformation of Ireland from an oral culture, in which storytelling provided a valid and important outlet for the narrative and poetic impulses of 'uneducated' people, to a literary one, was more-or-less complete by the 1970s. (Oral tradition had been thriving in certain Irish rural communities much later than in most other parts of Europe.) Less obvious influences on the emergence of writing as an art

15 See Diarmud Ferriter, *Ambiguous republic: Ireland in the 1970s* (London, 2012). 16 The influence on emerging writers of the revised English syllabus introduced in secondary schools in the mid-1960s, particularly the effect of Augustine Martin's short story anthology, *Exploring English 1*, was probably considerable. 17 It is not insignificant that the UCD Belfield campus, providing physical space for the thousands of students it would eventually contain, opened in 1970. The numbers of students in third-level education expanded rapidly in the 1970s. In 1971, there were 20,000 university students in Ireland (less than the total number in UCD in 2013, it is worth noting). But, by 1981, this figure had doubled. See Ferriter, *Ambiguous republic*, p. 634.

to which almost anyone could aspire were new publications. The 'New Irish Writing' page, introduced to the *Irish Press* in 1970 and edited for ten years by David Marcus, was pre-eminent among these, offering a regular outlet and creating a very large readership for new Irish writing and writers. But the establishment of new publishing houses – Poolbeg Press, Wolfhound Press, Attic Press and Arlen House – in this period also formed part of the wide picture. David Marcus, literary editor of the *Irish Press* and co-founder of the new Poolbeg Press, had close ties with Listowel Writers' Week – he adjudicated their short story competition and selected young writers for scholarships to attend its writing workshops. Arlen House, the feminist publishing imprint, set up its own series, the National Women's Writers Workshops, in the early 1980s, with the express purpose of nurturing new women writers. The Irish Writers' Centre, which had been run informally for some years by Jack Harte, was established as a formal institution, in premises on Parnell Square, in 1987. While serving many functions, the Centre, from its inception, offered a variety of courses on various aspects of creative writing, with its offerings becoming gradually more specialized and genre-focused.

It is against this complex cultural and social background, and during a vibrant, thrilling and indeed optimistic period of regeneration in Ireland, that the creative writing workshop found its first foothold, and that post-modern Irish literature, in its diversity of voices, genres and subject matter, has its origins. The courses and workshops mentioned here are only a few of those which flourished in Ireland in the 70s and 80s, and which were the forerunners of current academic programmes. The establishment of Creative Writing as an academic discipline has in no way diminished the role of non-academic institutions, organizations and groups, in providing opportunities for writers to meet, learn and discuss their work under the guidance of experienced practitioners.

Academia and the community meet very clearly in Trinity College, where the Writer in Residence at the Oscar Wilde Centre teaches students on the MPhil in Creative Writing programme and also runs a community workshop. That some academic programmes in Irish universities evolved from community-based courses is notable. In the case of University College Dublin, for instance, Dorothy Molloy Carpenter moderated extra-mural workshops and a vigorous poets' group, the Thornfield Poets, from the 1990s until her untimely death in 2004. In 2006, her husband, Andrew Carpenter, then Head of the School of English, Drama and Film, founded the MA in Creative Writing in UCD, a course which is still running successfully and which has been augmented by the recent MFA programme, inaugurated in 2011. In this instance, the link between the community and academic programme is very apparent. Similarly, in NUI Galway the academic MA in Writing evolved from the National Writers' Workshop.

The proliferation of graduate degree programmes, their popularity among students and the ease with which these programmes have been integrated into Irish universities – all under the auspices of departments of English – renders the perennial concern, 'can creative writing be taught?' obsolete.[18] Certain old-fashioned prejudices against the teaching of writing linger for reasons that are historically and psychologically interesting but require no elaboration here. The first response to the argument against teaching writing – based on largely unfounded romantic notions of creativity, and understandable fears that the imagination may be hampered by institutionalization and excessive editorial interference, or rules (views well expressed by Roddy Doyle in this collection) – is that the literary imagination is very robust. It survives in prisons and labour camps, and seems positively to thrive in hospitals. Universities seem like harmless enemies, by comparison with the gulag. The second response is that creative writing has been taught now for almost a hundred years in the United States, and that many of the greatest writers of the twentieth and twenty-first century are graduates of what Mark McGurl calls 'the program'.[19] Indeed, a significant sector of the most talented and significant mid-career Irish writers (Anne Enright, John Boyne, Glenn Patterson and Deirdre Madden) are graduates of Creative Writing programmes in the UK, while the emerging generation of Irish writers – Claire Kilroy, Claire Keegan, Susan Stairs, Jamie O'Connell, Colin Barrett, Alan Timmons and countless others – have studied Creative Writing in Irish universities.

The relevant questions for Ireland today are not 'Can creative

18 Departments of Irish have been slow to initiate degree programmes in Creative Writing, although unaccredited workshops and mentoring schemes for aspiring writers in Irish are occasionally offered, mainly outside of academia.   19 Mark McGurl, *The program era: postwar fiction and the rise of Creative Writing* (Cambridge, MA, 2009).

writing be taught?' but 'How is it taught?', 'How should it be taught?' 'What is best practice?' A need to find an answer, or answers, to the latter questions, was the driving energy of the symposium, How can it be taught?: Teaching and learning Creative Writing in Ireland, which was organized by the Royal Irish Academy, and took place in Academy House, Dublin, on 14 October 2011. Although Creative Writing is by now firmly established in the Irish university and community, those who design the curricula, teach, facilitate, supervise and grade, had seldom, if ever, gathered to share their ideas and experiences, either at a conference or in a volume, in Ireland. In the US and UK, conferences relating to creative writing in the academy are regular, and publications dealing with all aspects of the discipline in universities proliferate.[20] The Commitee for Irish Literatures in English believed it was timely to convene an event where teachers and writers from the many Irish universities, and from the other organizations and institutions involved in creative writing teaching, could assemble, and share their experiences with one another and an audience of interested writers. This volume contains articles that were in most instances first delivered as presentations at that symposium, as well as some additional essays, commissioned for the collection.

Teachers of creative writing, in Ireland as elsewhere, are writers themselves – just as teachers of most subjects in the university are scholars and researchers themselves, rather than people merely with pedagogical training. But while lecturers in subjects such as English or History, for example, learn to teach on the job, they have the advantage of having studied their subjects in the university; where their students sat, there they themselves sat, often not so very long before they took up their position on the lecturer's podium or behind the seminar leader's desk. While training for teaching in the academy is not mandatory, and, in Ireland, is often acquired voluntarily, models of university teaching are plentiful. This is not usually the case as far as the present generation of teachers of creative writing is concerned, simply because it is the first generation. As Mary Morrissy points out

---

20 The Great Writing Conference, organized by the University of Bangor, is a major annual event in the academic calendar in the UK. The Association of Writers and Writing Programs, AWP, holds annual conferences in the United States. Proceedings of these conferences are regularly published and there is a growing number of works treating the subject of the teaching of creative writing, including Paul Perry, *Beyond the workshop* (London, 2012).

in her article dealing with the problem of grading: 'As a self-taught writer, I had only attended one writers' workshop as a participant ... As a teacher, I was learning from my students the jargon for skills I had been using instinctively for years – motivation, back-story, point-of-view.'[21] Many teachers of Creative Writing in Irish universities at the moment, with the exception of a few who took the MFA abroad, find themselves in a similar position. They are instinctive writers, or perhaps more accurately, autodidacts, who have learnt by reading. In my case, although I had a degree in English (in common with many Irish writers), and had attended a few workshops as a young writer, I did not hear basic fictional concepts such as point of view and voice until a late stage in my career, much less discussed from a technical, moral or philosophical perspective. I learned by imitation and practice, as people of my father's generation learnt to drive, without the benefit of formal lessons or even a handbook outlining the rules of the road. Not only have most creative writing teachers in Ireland received no pedagogical training, they have never themselves studied the subject they teach in a formal academic setting. While it is generally accepted that only those who are themselves writers, preferably writers of some experience, are suited to teach, guide or supervise the writing of others, those writers who are chosen to teach or who elect to do so, are presented with a major challenge, in the first instance on a very practical level. It is a very simple one. *How* do you teach creative writing? It is one thing to write yourself, and to review or criticize the writing of others in a temporary, once-off, workshop situation, lasting for a couple of hours or, as it often is, a weekend. It is quite another to teach university courses of ten or twenty weeks' duration, leading to a Masters degree. What is the fellow, writer in residence, adjunct professor, or whatever she or he is called (usually something vague, indicating the as yet marginal status of Creative Writing and its teachers in the university – in itself a topic begging discussion) supposed to do, in her modules? At the crudest level, how does one fill the twenty or thirty teaching hours of the standard ten credit course? How are the ninety credits awarded to a Masters in Creative Writing calculated? How are degree curricula and individual module programmes in creative writing designed? What elements do they

21 See below p. 136.

contain? What should students, embarking on a Master's degree, expect to learn or experience, in return for their not-inconsiderable investment of time and money?

The traditional workshop established long ago, in which students present pieces of work for review by the class and by the teacher, may or may not be the best pedagogical model for the new Irish programmes. Flannery O'Connor, an Iowa graduate, expressed the caustic view that 'we can learn how *not* to write',[22] indicating that the workshop as defined and experienced by her was primarily editorial in approach. Today's students may demand and justifiably expect more than negative feedback. Paul Perry, in his article, explores the concept of the traditional workshop and offers imaginative ideas for its renewal and development. The question of how much space (or rather, time) is devoted to product-oriented teaching, in which information about, for example, craft or technique is offered, is ripe for discussion in the Irish context. That there should be a balance of studio-type, practical learning – that is, the writing workshop – and traditional academic learning, based on reading, analysis, learning, seems theoretically desirable. How can that balance be maintained? How does a moderator tally the obligation to encourage, inspire and nurture with the academic duty of criticism (and grading)? This issue is engagingly dealt with by Mary Morrissy.

Even before we address the kind of philosophical questions that engage American and British academics in this field, relating to the effects of academic institutionalization on the individual creativity of the writer, the precious self (of either student or teacher) and the impact creative writing programmes have on the national literature, we in Ireland need to discover what *actually happens* in our Creative Writing classes. An Irish Creative Writing pedagogue may find the kind of anxiety American commentators suffer about the risks of the lifeless 'MFA story' or 'Campus Novel' a bit of an academic luxury, since she probably has no idea what goes on in any Creative Writing classroom apart from her own. If the Irish teaching practices are in fact uniform, that has come about entirely by accident.

A considerable literature on the theory and practice of Creative Writing pedagogy, produced in the US and the UK, is available to the

---

22 Cited in McGurl, *The program era*, p. 131.

Irish teacher of Creative Writing – much of it excellent. Intercollegiate discussion, debate and critique are needed to ensure wise selection of such reading material, for staff and students alike, and to build up good collections of significant books in university libraries.

Ireland is in a fortunate position, as far as Creative Writing is concerned, poised on a peak with a clear view of the sunlit American landscape of previous Creative Writing programmes and an inevitably dimmer outlook over the misty landscape of the future of the programmes in Ireland. We need to clear some of that Irish fog. On the one hand, we may draw on the experience of the United States and the UK, as we strive to create excellent academic programmes for this subject here. On the other, we are unhampered by established traditions of pedagogy in the field in our own country. The Creative Writing project in Ireland is fired by the energy that inspires all novel enterprises. We are free to explore ways of teaching and learning Creative Writing, to design curricula which benefit from the long-established experiences of other countries, but which can develop in entirely new ways, suited to the particular Irish literary context. That for the past fifteen years or so we have allowed the subject to evolve and grow untrammelled by excessive organization or debate is probably positive. There is a spontaneity in it which matches that of the 'program' in the United States in its embryonic form, eighty years ago. But we are also in a position to learn from the experience of others, and to plan accordingly.

Mark McGurl, in his analysis of the Creative Writing project in the United States, observes that 'the rise of the creative writing program stands as the most important event in postwar American literary history, and that paying attention to the increasingly intimate relation between literary production and the practices of higher education is the key to understanding the originality of postwar American fiction.'[23] That there has for long been a connection between university education and literature in Ireland is beyond dispute. Two of our great classics – James Joyce's *A portrait of the artist as a young man* and Flann O'Brien's *At Swim-two-birds* – are, if not campus novels, then student novels, and directly influenced both by the university-life experiences and university reading of their authors. The impact of the expansion of third-level

23 McGurl, *The program era*, p. ix.

education in Ireland from the 1970s on Irish literature has been immense, and the influence of the reading and literary analysis undertaken in university literature curricula, particularly in English and Irish departments, on Irish writing is, undoubtedly, significant, given that many, indeed, probably the majority, of contemporary writers in Ireland have taken degrees in literature, in the absence, until recently, of degrees in Creative Writing as such. It is certain that the new Creative Writing degree courses will exercise a strong influence on the writers of the future and the work they produce – that is, on the literature of Ireland. It is important, therefore, that due consideration is given to how these programmes are designed and delivered, and desirable that the by now large community of Creative Writing teachers should share their experiences, opinions, philosophies, hopes and methodologies, with a view to achieving the best possible learning environments for their students.

The first draft of the Creative Writing programme in Ireland has been written. It is now time to cast a critical eye on the text that has been generated in a spirit of creative spontaneity. It is essential that we edit and discard, develop and expand. It is time to think seriously about what we are doing, since the late starter, Creative Writing, is one of the most popular subjects in our universities, and has the potential to become absolutely central to the humanities and wider afield. Creative Writing, in its broadest sense, is one of the foundation stones of the university – how it relates to its equally essential companion, critical writing, is one of the fundamental questions not just for creative writing programmes, but for all university disciplines.

The initial essays in this volume by Gerald Dawe and Roddy Doyle document the evolution of the teaching of Creative Writing in Ireland in the academy and the community and comment on the possible tensions as well as interconnections between the two domains. While Dawe is sanguine about the possibility of teaching Creative Writing in the university, Doyle is wary of the negative impact of imposing constraints, especially on young writers, even in the most open of community-based facilities. Paul Perry, for his part, weighs up the debate concerning the usefulness of the workshop model, and proposes that the workshop can indeed be a nurturing and evolving space that fosters growth and not just a mechanism for inducing uniformity as its detractors gloomily insist.

Practical advice on how to teach is offered in several articles. Sinéad Morrissey lists what it is not possible to teach: talent, intelligence and inspiration. (Presumably it's impossible to teach the first two to students of medicine or engineering either.) She goes on to delineate the many skills which are equally important for the poet, and which can be taught. In this essay, the irritating question of the romantic school of amateurism, which refuses to recognize that Creative Writing can be taught, is neatly tucked up in bed and sent soundly to sleep. Nessa O'Mahony delineates how Creative Writing is effectively taught in online courses but details how teachers have to work to counteract the anonymity and brashness of peer review that is effected through email exchanges. She also notes, however, that digital communication has many advantages and that it can promote open exchange about the experience of writing through shared postings in dedicated chatrooms and noticeboards. Éilís Ní Dhuibhne tackles the quandary facing instructors who propose to teach the novel in Creative Writing programmes and notes the paradox that novels, no matter how much time is allotted to their consideration, can only ever be examined partially or in installments. For all the insouciance with which self-help manuals offer guidelines on novel writing and breezily assume a speedy process of composition, achieving a vantage point from which to assess the overall effects aimed at by the apprentice author of a novel remains, in her eyes, one of the principal challenges facing the teacher and student of Creative Writing alike. Mary Morrissy broaches a further set of intractable issues in looking at the seeming mismatch between the purported aim to nurture creativity, on the one hand, and the unbending requirement to grade students' work, on the other. Soberingly, she unpicks the mixed motives that may inform the experience of grading whereby the instructor, far from being impartial, may find herself acting like a would-be publisher with an appraising eye for marketability or falling back on the imprecise and dubious standards of personal taste.

The peculiar and vexed role of personal experience in sustaining and inspiring creative writing is a topic treated in several of the essays. Both Carlo Gébler and Eibhear Walshe consider the genre of life writing and outline the serendipitous ways in which they began to write in this field. They acknowledge the roots of such work in autobiographical experience but also stress the need to achieve a distance from it and to recast it imaginatively. Mary O'Donnell points to the dangers of equating veracity with sincerity or indeed of allowing personal emotion too large a space in the workshop or assuming that it is a hallmark of a well-written text. For her, patience, the measured application of time and the constant stepping back from drafts of work in order to revise them are essential aspects of learning the craft of writing and propensities that the Creative Writing teacher endeavours to inculcate above all else.

A number of contributors to the collection point to the dangers the modern literary scene poses for serious writers, and for literature overall. Celebrity culture can be the enemy of good writing, and suggest to young authors that their only object is worldly success. Academic programmes in creative writing offer writers a temporary refuge from such venality and create a space in which excellent writing, rather than fame, is central; in this protective sphere the young, or not-so-young apprentice, can enjoy the chance to develop as a person, and to hone her or his craft. Moreover, several contributors, including Leanne O'Sullivan and Mary O'Donnell, attest to the key role that the workshop experience played in setting them on the path of becoming authors. Vitally, O'Donnell highlights the importance of workshops for the launching of the careers of women writers in the 1970s and 1980s in Ireland, while O'Sullivan writes movingly about how she learnt to become a writer and subsequently a teacher through her experiences in the classroom. The formative nature of the workshop, for all its haphazardness and informality, is a consistent feature of writer's biographies. It is to be expected that the mentoring and shaping function of creative writing programmes will have an even more enduring role to play in the future, given their current embeddedness in Irish universities and the increasing numbers of graduates they are producing.

Sinéad Morrissey mentions that the degree course is only the first step on a long road for the serious writer. This is indeed true, and all the more reason for those who are the keepers of creative writing programmes to reflect carefully on how they are preparing their students for the wonderful journey ahead.

This volume represents a first selection of reflections, reports, recommendations and thoughts of Irish teachers of Creative Writing on their work. The wide variety of techniques, questions and observations contained within these covers offers an inkling of how nuanced and many-faceted the subject we call Creative Writing is. The symposium that gave rise to this book was designed as a space in which practitioners could come together to share techniques and experiences and to learn from one another. Creative writing workshops, courses and degree programmes, among other things, inculcate in students the ability to take a critical stance in relation to their own work and that of others. While not losing the magic or alchemical factor, the kindling spark that fires all creative endeavours, they become reflective, and aware of what they are doing. Such a critical stance is also needed in relation to the practice of the teaching of Creative Writing in Ireland. In openly canvassing their views and experiences and sharing their prized pedagogical strategies as well as their professional misgivings, the contributors to this collection have, not only provided an invaluable overview of the state of the discipline in the country, but also undertaken in many instances a critique of many of its cherished principles and presumptions.

The history and practice of the teaching of creative writing in Ireland

GERALD DAWE

In April 1976, the playwright and novelist, Thomas Kilroy, published an account of an experiment which had just concluded in Galway.[1] The experiment was a ten-week course for writers based in University College Galway (as it then was known). The National Writers' Workshop, sponsored by the Arts Council of Ireland, was the first of its kind. According to an earlier report by Michael Finlan, which had marked the beginning of the venture in January that year, the idea for the course had come from novelist Éilís Dillon.[2] Future moderators based at UCG would include Eoghan Ó Tuairisc, John McGahern and Patrick Mason and in many ways it was the prototype for creative writing programmes in this country.

In his retrospective, Kilroy was of the opinion that the experiment had worked:

> It is difficult to give an adequate impression of that discussion: explication, analysis, criticism, certainly but also the opening up and defining of the personality through the medium of highly personal work. We covered an extraordinary amount of material and in depth.[3]

Kilroy went on to generalize about his experience of the writers' group in terms which I think are possibly even more relevant today:

> As a writer I was interested in this course because of my belief in the importance of a critical intelligence operating within imaginative writing. Despite the exceptional imaginative energy in Irish writing, now and in the past, we have never had what might be called a critical tradition in our culture. The absence of a tradition of enquiry and analysis has influenced not only the

---

[1] Thomas Kilroy, 'The Writers' Group in Galway', *Irish Times,* 8 April 1976, p. 10.
[2] Michael Finlan, 'Ten-Week Course for Writers opens in UCG', *Irish Times*, 19 January 1976, p. 11.   [3] Thomas Kilroy, 'The Writers' Group in Galway', p. 10.

shape of our art but the nature of our politics, our religious practices, our social habits, I believe, in a way that has seriously diminished their potential.[4]

In the thirty-five years that separate us from that early exercise, the situation has completely changed in what is now generally referred to as creative writing (a phrase absent from Kilroy's article). Apart from the pioneering work of the Poet's House, based at one time in the North of Ireland with a degree course accredited by a UK university, Trinity College Dublin was the first Irish university to offer a Masters programme in Creative Writing in 1998. Several other Irish universities have since followed on with fully accredited degrees in Creative Writing and/or publishing and editing, at both undergraduate and graduate levels. However, it should be noted that Creative Writing workshops had proliferated and developed from the 1960s and the early 1970s, both informally and formally.[5] The universities were merely catching up with developments already taking place in the wider society and responded accordingly.

My own anecdotal sense of this growth is aligned to initiatives in Irish state policy, with leadership from the Arts Councils in both parts of the island, in the form of the 'Writers-in-Schools' scheme, supplemented by the 'Writers-in-Prisons' scheme, established under the guidance of Brendan Kennelly.[6] Both initiatives flourished during the 1980s and 1990s and continue to play an important (if largely unheralded) role in Irish cultural life. The innovative drive of numerous women's groups is also a key part of this story in that the hard-won struggle for various civic rights was responsive to a deep need for a breakthrough in establishing platforms for woman's writing, fostered by Eavan Boland among many others.

Since these developments took place, non-academic creative writing courses, based in literature centres and libraries, have sprung up all over the country, including Dublin, Cork and Galway, engaging with

---

4 Ibid., p. 10.   5 One such instance was the 'Group' of Northern poets at Queen's University Belfast which met under moderator Philip Hobsbaum. See Heather Clarke, 'The Belfast Group', *The Ulster Renaissance: poetry in Belfast, 1962–1972* (Oxford, 2006), pp 43–71.   6 See www.poetryireland.ie/education/writers-in-schools.html, accessed 10 July 2013. In 1986, the School of English, Trinity College Dublin, in association with the Arts Council of Ireland established the Irish Writer Fellowship with Derek Mahon as the inaugural Fellow. See http://www.tcd.ie/OWC/writers/past-fellow.php, accessed 10 July 2013.

new important challenges in Irish society, such as the Fighting Words initiative in Dublin.[7] There are Creative Writing networks and dedicated writers' groups that meet in local neighbourhoods in numerous villages, towns and cities. Alongside which, there are now workshops attached to literary festivals and creative writing residential weekends. Creative Writing courses are offered by national newspapers, literary magazines and local versions of UK-based publishers have included in recent years academy-style programmes – many of which are run on commercial bases.

In Ireland today, there is a lot of Creative Writing going on, at all kinds of levels and with different scales of expectation and provision, obviously not just in the universities. There are some who find all this Creative Writing buzz less than convincing, being of the opinion that while it does not do any harm, it bears little critical relationship to actual literary production and achievement or the essentially self-motivated, solitary and singular nature of the artistic personality. Others may be of the view that the *non-academic* Creative Writing experience is closer to ordinary reality and, as a result, more valid and praiseworthy as a form for individual or social expression, prioritizing the building of self-esteem over other literary objectives.

There are those who consider that the involvement of the academy, through the accreditation of degrees in Creative Writing, will inevitably lead us in Ireland towards the kind of parallel universe in which students enroll primarily to become teachers of Creative Writing rather than to become bolder and better poets, fiction writers and playwrights with working lives outside the Creative Writing hub. While there are academics and writers who remain less than enamoured with the Creative Writing project the demand for such courses is steady and shows no sign of diminishing in the years ahead.

The question has to be asked: what is Creative Writing as an academic discipline? Is it literature, and if so, what criteria do or should we use to teach it, or assess it? There is also the seemingly unpreventable question that emerges when Creative Writing as a concept enters the air space of the media: Is it possible to teach someone how to be a writer? This question seems – to me at least – wilfully to ignore the guilds and *ad hoc* groups and patronage systems

---

7 See http://www.fightingwords.ie, accessed 10 July 2013 and Roddy Doyle, below, pp 35–44.

through which artists, musicians, theatre practitioners and writers have for centuries past shared their practical skills. From another strictly educational viewpoint, questions can be raised about whether or not it is pedagogically sensible for a poet or novelist or playwright, who may have displayed little previous aptitude, appetite or skill, to be in charge of a class simply *because* he or she is a writer. And there is too the complicated situation of an individual writer who may well find the year-long business of teaching, assessment, administration and pastoral concerns, a testing burden on the real work at hand – his or her own writing – and a difficult and sometimes stressful balance to achieve.

There is also the consideration that, while an individual artist may not indeed be a great teacher, his or her depth of learning and range of experience as a writer brings its own lasting inspiration and educational value. It would be a pity if idiosyncrasy and unpredictability – often the hallmarks of the creative mind – were ruled out of the classroom in the interests of bland routine. Genuine creativity can be wayward, a point that can pass the cultural legislators by. There is too the wider history and culture of the writer based in the university Creative Writing system – a cultural history only beginning in Ireland yet one that has fascinating historical roots. It is a system much influenced by the example and protocols of writing programmes in the United States.

An established and respected American poet, Louis Simpson, reflected in 1991 on his time teaching mainly in university poetry workshops:

> The students I had were amazingly ignorant. They wanted to write poetry because they were far more interested in their own feelings than in the feelings of other people ... They knew hardly anything of history, philosophy or religion. What they did know about was writing as a career – the names of successful poets were often on their lips, the ones who were awarded prizes and who frequently gave poetry readings. The writing students were blown about by every wave of fashion.[8]

---

8 Louis Simpson, 'On the neglect of poetry in the United States' in *Ships going into the blue: essays and notes on poetry* (Ann Arbor, 1994), p. 88.

I don't think this is where we are in Ireland but it is a timely warning of where we could be heading unless different kinds of artistic and cultural motivations are fashioned in our own context to provide a more complex and challenging educational experience for future generations. We obviously have to think here about quality and excellence, and about critical and technical standards when we talk about creativity as well as the issues of equality of opportunity and access in social terms.

The 'subculture' that Louis Simpson caricatures is something akin to a form of literary *X-Factor*[9] and it may not be completely unfamiliar to those involved in literary matters in Ireland. More pertinently, Simpson goes on to remark of the process of assessment, 'A teacher of creative writing is expected to encourage students [which is] a very different thing than giving honest criticism'.[10] Another American poet, Elizabeth Bishop, remarked in 1966: 'if *anyone* in that class uses the word "communicate" *once* more, I'm going to *scream*! I *hate* that word. Those students are *not* there to "express" themselves; they're there to learn how to write a *good poem*.'[11]

While these American considerations may not have the same voltage in the particular contexts of the Irish literary or academic world of Creative Writing, both Simpson and Bishop raise an important pedagogical issue about what it is Creative Writing *teaches*; or to put this another way, what do we do when we teach 'it'. For me there is no mystery here. Creative writing is a generic term which has international name-recognition for those who want to develop their skills at writing poetry, fiction, drama and non-fiction. But as a subject or academic discipline it evaporates in my mind. I don't think it exists at all and believe that the Creative Writing culture is something we should be very circumspect about building into a virtual reality distinct from the actual demands of the literary world. The whole point of teaching Creative Writing – in whatever setting – is to benefit the individual and strengthen his or her ability to read and see better what it is he or she is

---

9 Even though the context is poetry in the United States, Simpson's remarks are worth quoting in full: 'Yes, many books of verse are published in the States every year, and many poetry readings are taking place, mostly on college campuses. On the other hand, the books are read by no one but poets and would-be poets, and the audiences at readings are composed of the same people, those who have a professional interest in poetry, that is, poetry as a means of getting a job ... teaching "creative writing"', 'On the neglect of poetry in the United States', p. 85.   10 Ibid., p. 87.   11 See George Monteiro (ed.), *Conversations with Elizabeth Bishop* (Jackson, 1996), p. 38.

doing; to critically connect the reality of the poem or story or scene from a play with the aspiration of the writer; and to place in a revealing light what has or has not been achieved. Knowledge, example, comparisons that flow from the imaginative use of language, are every bit as critical as the support and responses of encouragement and enjoyment. And we cannot exclude the pleasure principle in all this; otherwise, why bother?

The role of Creative Writing should not in my opinion be the equivalent of a feel-good session of self congratulation. Vigorous reading and revision need to be adjusted obviously to the particular setting but my own sense of Creative Writing is that it is only about one thing and one thing alone: practice, the making of literary work. In order for this to be achieved individuals – in community workshops as much as in seminar rooms – need to think about what they are doing, and to be challenged to do better, and to learn as much as they can about the making of literature from various traditions other than their own in time and place. This assumes a certain degree of enthusiasm, engagement, belief and knowledge, of course, but when it is matched with intrinsic talent and focus, the work will prosper. Whether this will add up to literary success is, of course, another day's work.

In terms of my own experience, it seems incontrovertible that best practice comes from the workshop when it is being conducted as precisely that – a *work* shop. Obviously this has to be supplemented for those who want their writing to become a way of life with a realistic picture of the publishing world, of the business (to quote Louis Simpson again) of 'making a name and getting ahead' and of the varied personal and professional pressures of 'being a writer'.[12] My sense of creative writing is predicated exclusively upon the individual's expectations, not upon the putative function of Creative Writing as a subject in itself. I find such intellectualizing and problematizing a side-show. The delivery of a class – the pedagogy of what happens in Creative Writing workshops – is not structurally different from the rehearsal of a scene in a play, the practice of a pianist or dancer or, for that matter, the intensity of a good sophister or graduate literature seminar at full tilt.

Yet, I would like to refer to two related articles on the subject of Creative Writing that in one way or another raise intellectual questions about the value and moral dimensions of long-established Creative

---

12 Simpson, 'Theater business', *Ships going into the blue*, p. 41.

Writing programmes in the States. As a background note of reference to this collection of essays on the Irish experience, they are apt. The first is a lengthy review article by Elif Batuman, published in the *London Review of Books,* to which the novelist Paul Murray drew my attention when he was Visiting Writer Fellow at the Oscar Wilde Centre at Trinity College Dublin.¹³ The second is an essay by Louis Menand, 'Show and tell: should creative writing be taught?', published in the *New Yorker.*¹⁴ Both articles respond to Mark McGurl's study, *The program era: postwar fiction and the role of creative writing.*¹⁵ I think I am right in saying that the answer to the question posed by Menand is: yes, creative writing should be taught. But we have to watch out for the pitfalls, excesses and failures of critical judgement that Batuman identifies in the US system. She castigates the wound culture within which creative writing is all too often identified as a form of compensation and questions the propensity of writers to enter the literary market via prestigious Creative Writing schools as a form of self-commodification.¹⁶ Batuman is particularly alarmed by what McGurl describes as the role of 'paradoxically *enabling* disablement'¹⁷ and also challenges both 'literary production as social advocacy'¹⁸ and 'fiction as a form of empathy training':

> Although there is nothing wrong with writing about persecution, for either the persecuted or the non-persecuted, there is a genuine problem when young people are taught to believe that they can be writers only in the presence of real or invented socio-political grievances.¹⁹

She queries how in the handbook-driven, manual-conscious, American environment of many deterministic Creative Writing programmes – understandably reacting in part to the more informal, therapeutic workshop – students and their teachers become obsessed by technique and writing exercises. She notes that the 'raw material hardly seems to matter anymore ... The fetishization of technique simultaneously

---

13 Elif Batuman, 'Get a real degree', *London Review of Books*, 32 (2010), 3–8. 14 Louis Menand, 'A critic at large: show or tell: should creative writing be taught?', *New Yorker,* 8 and 15 June 2009. 15 Mark McGurl, *The program era: postwar fiction and the role of creative writing* (Cambridge, 2009). 16 Batuman, 'Get a real degree', p. 7. 17 Ibid. 18 Ibid., p. 11. 19 Ibid.

assuages and aggravates the anxiety that literature might not be real work'.[20] The conclusive point that Batuman reaches is a somewhat absolutist, exasperated hope that Creative Writing programmes should 'teach writers about history and the world, and not just about adverbs and themselves'.[21] She does not seem to entertain the possibility that 'the world and history' might well be elliptically contained in an 'adverb'.

Batuman's view is corroborated by Louis Menand in his response to the McGurl book, which also provides a useful mini-history of the American experience, identifying many of its successes and strengths but also illustrating the psychological weaknesses, indulgences and ego-driven problematic that have obtained from time to time. 'Surely the goal should be', Menard asks, 'to get people to learn to think while they're writing, not after they have written'.[22] In saying so, he stresses the key elements of 'revision', 'the importance of making things', 'a love of reading' and of 'moving in the world' before concluding in the workshop of his own remembering:

> I don't think the workshops taught me too much about craft, but they did teach me about the importance of making things, not just reading things. You care about things you make, and that makes it easier to care about things that other people make.[23]

If Creative Writing in Ireland 'makes it easier to care about things that other people make' then that is a very good place from which to start – which neatly brings us back to Thomas Kilroy's observations in 1976 about the need for a critical spirit to match the imaginative energy, to foster and guide writers through the courses that many gifted and committed authors and academics offer – Creative Writing programmes, workshops, call them what you will. Kilroy's emphasis on the role of critical intelligence and the need for enquiry and analysis are fundamental here.

In the period of time that separates us from Kilroy's original comments, the sheer volume of material in English that is now produced internationally – in print books and online – make it near-on

---

20 Ibid., p. 12. 21 Ibid., p. 15. 22 Menand, 'A critic at large', p. 111. 23 Ibid., p. 112.

impossible to maintain any degree of critical focus in the public perception and reception of literary writing. The mass market bookselling world of wall-to-wall exposure and publicity book tours have brought literature ever closer to entertainment. Self-parody seems to merge with self-importance in the profiles that have largely taken the place of intelligent readings of a writer's work as critical proportion and historical comparison are becoming much less securely based upon shared literary values of a sophisticated literary discourse.

Louis Simpson was unequivocal on this point as it related to the world of poetry as he experienced it twenty years ago:

> But then you have to think that poetry is an art, and that the poet aims to make it grow. If you conceive of poetry as entertainment, which is what reaching out for a wider audience requires, then by all means do everything you can to increase your audience. But will it be an audience for poetry or for theatrics – an attractive personality, a striking emotional delivery? The people who would rather have their poetry in performance are not lovers of poetry but of performance.[24]

Or maybe they are lovers of both? Either way, the over-arching notion of celebrity in today's culture has weakened the moral authority of the writer and his or her place as a genuinely independent figure on the critical edge of the mainstream. Modern literature has always had its celebrities (think of Dickens) but they were better known for the views and visions their writing embodied than for their lifestyles and the foibles of their personalities which is increasingly more the case. It is not that the process of promotion is at fault – the greater and wider access to writers and writing is a certain good – but rather that the product that fits this process best tends to be based on what the market can sell rather than on literary excellence. The saturation of the media with populist notions of accessibility contrasts with the increasingly diminished role of literary reviewing as a form of critical filter and opinion-making. These influences have had a huge impact on how literary writing in Ireland, the UK and North America is viewed. As writing itself is turned more publically into a lifestyle choice driven by

---

24 Simpson, 'On the neglect of poetry in the United States', p. 91.

the promise of some degree of commercial and/or emotional reward, being a novelist sounds roughly the same as being a chef.

It is in such circumstances as these that Creative Writing, both in the academy and without, finds its pedagogical, commercial and cultural *raison d'être*. Writing is seen more popularly as an option and the inclusivity of creativity in the face of economic recession is portrayed as a key to innovation and self-esteem. Viewing writing as a cultural entitlement shifts the balance significantly away from innate individual talent to something viewed as an access route ('a journey') to self-expression which can then in turn weaken our understanding of literary value and detach our reading of an author's work from any critical understanding of his/her formal achievement in the use of language. The pre-eminent view of the social benefits of literature is equally promoted as a non-judgemental communicator of class, gender and ethnicity issues and valuable primarily in these terms alone.

These current characteristics have created in turn a different kind of audience with a different set of aspirations and expectations, a niche-market of genre writing, which has and will continue materially to affect the way literature is read and, of course, taught. It has always been this way – the history of literary fashion is scored with fads as any research through the best-selling lists of the 1910s, 1920s or 1930s will show. But what has altered in the present is the rapid technological developments of e-books and Kindles, the upsurge in festivals and literary events and the significance of marketing for publishing and book-selling. Those engaged in creative writing need to know just how much of the visibility of their writing will be utterly dependent upon the non-creative realities of publishing and that that reality check can be chastening. Ironically, in this context, Creative Writing may become a crucial point of critical reference and relevance as the market place seeks ever more product to *buy* and also as the pressure of selling grows increasingly influential in defining our literary culture – in much the same way as these factors have impacted upon other cultural sectors such as popular music.

We are all in this world ourselves – as writers both in and out of the academy. Maybe the academy, the much-derided ivory tower (a silly patronizing phrase for intellectual and imaginative effort), will provide a haven in the twenty-first century within which the artistic imagination finds time and space to prosper and wherein the craft of writing will be able to thrive in the free if challenging atmosphere of critical exchange – practices for which the great universities were originally built.

Write first, worry later: fostering creativity in the classroom

RODDY DOYLE

Some years ago, I sat in Fighting Words, a writing centre for children and young people, in Dublin, and watched a class of nine-year-old girls as they wrote a story, together. They sat on little beanbags, in front of a big screen. The screen was blank.

'What do all good stories have?' the adult standing in front of them asked.

The answers flew at her.

'Characters.'

'Things that are funny.'

'Full stops!'

One girl waved her hand in the air.

'Conflict and resolution,' she said.

It was a lovely moment. The adults in the room smiled and looked at one another, pleased to be in the company of such brightness. The girl's classmates ooohed, and smiled at their friend. That girl, those kids, were in good hands. Their teacher had written those words – 'conflict', 'resolution' – on the board. The children had learnt what they meant. Or, at least the girl with the waving hand had. They'd probably talked about them, and given examples of films they'd seen and stories they'd read.

Yet, a few minutes later, thinking about what I'd just witnessed, I felt less elated. I'd witnessed a very bright child, in a room full of bright children, telling us all that she'd been taught that what all stories have – must have – *are* – conflict and resolution, and this, I thought, was a pity. A pity that the child had been told the ingredients of a story, or how a story must be constructed, before she'd had a chance to write a story herself and make her own discoveries.

I don't for a minute think that the demands of the words 'conflict' and 'resolution' will slow down or impede that particular girl, no more than punctuation and grammar will. But they won't help either. And they will slow down, even turn off, other children – and adults.

'It's too hard.'

'I can't think of anything.'

Yet, since then, I've seen the words 'conflict' and 'resolution' in classrooms, on posters and boards. It's official – and it's the death of creativity before it even starts. It's the exam system and the fear of failure that paralyse innovation; the stupid insistence that everything worth learning or knowing can – and must – be measured objectively, that nothing is of value if it can't be measured in points and bonus points.

The thinking seems to be, a child can't write a short story until he knows what a short story is. But if we give a child a ball we don't insist that she learn the rules of association football before we'll let her kick it. Famously, when Everton's manager, David Moyes, went to the house where sixteen-year-old Wayne Rooney lived with his parents, after Wayne had become an immediate household name after scoring against Arsenal earlier that day, he found Wayne outside in the dark, alone, kicking a ball against a wall. That was what had made Rooney – the joy of the kick, the smack of the ball, the ability to make it come back to him. Everything else – the skill, the speed, the anticipation, aggression – these came later. The offside rule is vital. Without it, football as many of us know and love it, would stop. With it, if insisted upon too early, football would never start. Just give the kid the ball. The offside rule can come later.

The football analogy is, admittedly, a little forced.

'Just give the kid the car keys; he can pick it up as he goes along.'

But I think the same broad rule applies: give the child the freedom of the field or page, then take some of it back. Planning, thinking ahead, is good, to be encouraged. But too much of it can kill.

What the children in front of the screen at Fighting Words need – *all* they need – at the start is encouragement. That should go without saying and, in almost all senses, it does go without saying. No one in the room – in any room – wants the children to be discouraged, or frightened, to hide behind boredom, to turn off. There are the usual impediments – commas, apostrophes, spellings. Some children need to be assured that spellings don't matter, at first. Others won't go a word further until they are assured that a particular word is spelt correctly. For them, spelling is vital. And they're right. Spelling doesn't matter; spelling matters. Different messages, but the same message: 'You're great, keep going.'

A Junior Cert student recently told me that she hated 'personal writing'. I asked her why. 'Because we don't get enough time,' she said. She was referring to the Junior Cert English exam question. Her teacher had advised her not to opt for the short story; she wouldn't have time to write a good one properly and, anyway, it was too hard to mark.

School is all about time, chunks of measured time; the start of the day, and the bells within the day, the week, term, the year, the move from primary to secondary, the important examination years, time measured as investment in the future. It's a huge part of a good education: 'Don't waste time.' But a kid writing a story should be able to climb into a different kind of time. The page can also be seen as a form of time, measured across and down, and the move from one page to the next. But it isn't tick-tock time and it shouldn't be stopped by the bell or squashed into an exam paper.

I've heard children being told that they must know everything about a character before they start writing about that character, everything from ancestry to eye colour. But how much fun is that? Or how helpful? Must you know everything about that girl over there before you ask her up to dance? Must you know everything about your unborn baby's future before you agree to be its mother?

When I wrote my first novel, *The Commitments*, I gave the protagonist, Jimmy Rabbitte, a sister called Sharon. I didn't know he had a sister until he needed one, and he needed one because I wanted her to say 'Go and shite' as she was coming down the stairs to another character, Deco Cuffe, as he was going up the stairs. A year later, when I started *The Snapper*, a novel about a young woman who is pregnant, Sharon was the young woman, the protagonist, but only because she'd said 'Go and shite' to Deco Cuffe in the earlier book, and only because that had seemed like a good idea on the day I wrote it. When I was writing *A star called Henry*, I gave the protagonist, Henry Smart, blue eyes one day, months into the writing, because it became important that day, at that moment, that he had eyes and that they had a colour. I wrote a book for young people, called *A greyhound of a girl*. The first greyhound came into the story several months into the writing, as I dredged my childhood memories of visits to the farm where my grandfather grew up, and I remembered how the greyhounds had frightened me. So, in they went. Months after that, I made the protagonist's grandmother, a tall woman called Emer, call herself a 'greyhound of a girl'. I could make her say that because the story now had greyhounds. And that phrase became the book's title – months after the book was finished. The book's plot is held together by 'back-story' – glimpses of the past. The book makes no sense without them. But back story and the insistence on overly detailed character information – these are barbs on the barbed-wire fence, like spelling and punctuation, stopping the child from getting to the story. These things stop people from starting.

Back to the children on the beanbags, in Fighting Words. We want to encourage them to write. Before we set down rules or give advice, we invite them to put down words, then to add words to those words, to start assembling a story. But, of course, the blank white page is often a terrifying thing. The urge to fill it or the refusal to have anything to do with it – both extremes expose so much. What's good, what's wrong, what's correct, what's funny. Some children almost encircle the sheet of paper on the table; their arms go around it, as if they're dancing with it, falling in love. Others sit petrified, and stay petrified long after they leave school. We want to encourage these children to write, not terrify them.

When they arrived at Fighting Words, before they got to the beanbags, they were met at the front door and photographed. They were given name tags. They were excited; it was a morning off school. But they were also a bit puzzled. They knew they'd come to this place to write a story but the place was actually very small. There was only one desk and a long row of bookshelves. But then, once they'd all been photographed, the first piece of magic occurred. An adult – a Fighting Words volunteer – asked them to lean against a bookshelf, and it swung open. It was actually a hidden door, and now they saw the bigger room, the *real* room, the screen and the bean-bags. It began to make more sense. (The hidden door always works. Even twelve-year-old girls, wearing eye-liner, just weeks from the end of primary school, go 'ooh' when the door swings open.)

Now they're sitting in front of the screen which, except for the name of their school and class, is blank. The screen, for now, is the page. They're sitting together. They don't have to spell, yet. They don't have to hold a pen over the whiteness, yet. There's a volunteer sitting at a laptop, beside the screen, ready to write their words. There's another volunteer at the other side of the screen, an artist, standing at an easel, ready to draw the characters that the kids will soon invent. There's a third volunteer in front of the screen, in front of the children.

The invitation, 'Write anything you want', frightens even professional writers. So, to encourage the young writers, the volunteer in front of the screen asks a question.

'What do all good stories have?'

'Scary things!'

'Full stops!'

'Conflict and resolution.'

'Characters.'

Encouraged by the Fighting Words volunteer, the children choose a main character. They make a list of possible candidates. Sharks, pigs, doughnuts, leprechauns, gorilla boys. Bananas are popular. The one rule is that the characters must be original, invented in the room. There's a closed-eye vote to decide on the character. By the time the vote is over, the main character has been selected and the cheering has died down, the kids are already feeling proprietorial. They go through the same routine as they vote for the character's best friend, the character's greatest wish and greatest fear. They're ready to start – they've already started.

But before they get going, they're introduced to one more character, the editor, a cranky woman or man called, depending on which staff member is behind the wall in the Fighting Words office that particular morning, Missus, or Mister, McConkey. McConkey doesn't think that children can write good stories, hates being interrupted, and threatens to sack the volunteer if the kids don't come up with a good story. McConkey is always a hit. He, or she, has often become a character in the stories that the children start to write. Small children shout back at her, roaring their determination to write a masterpiece. Older boys and girls shout back too.

So, the kids start to compose the story, together.

Here are some of the more recent opening sentences:

'A long time ago in Pig World there lived a pig called Kate the Popular.'

'Tommy the Chainsaw woke up in his shed.'

'Once upon a time, there was a cheeseburger called Ham who was thinking of taking over the world.'

The first sentence, initially the idea of one child, but added to and debated, is typed onto the screen and the story starts to take shape.

They love to see the words – their words – go up on the screen. It's a simple, everyday event, but it always seems to be a novelty.

While the story starts to fill the page, the artist draws the first of three illustrations inspired by the characters and the plot, as it unfolds. Ideas grow, and change; the words become a story. The session lasts two hours and at some point, usually about an hour, the volunteer leading the exercise brings the on-screen part of the job to a halt, at a cliffhanger, some obvious place to stop.

The children move to tables and continue to write the story, this time using their own words. There is at least one volunteer at each table, encouraging the children, helping with spelling, if wanted, sometimes just sitting there and smiling, other times writing the words that the child delivers. While the children write their own conclusions, the on-screen section is printed, with the three illustrations, and stapled into simple book form, with cover, author photograph and blank pages so the children can write in their own endings.

About ten minutes before the end of the two hours, the kids stop writing. They move to the hatch in the office wall, from which McConkey's voice will pour.

They sit, and they wait.

McConkey is summoned. She – he – gives out. She's been busy paring her toenails. He's been cutting his nasal hair – something suitably disgusting. The kids' stories are sent through the hatch. McConkey reads the group-written part of the story, and then goes on to read some of the individual endings, out loud. He – she – has changed his mind. Children *can* write stories. Each child goes home with his or her own book. Excluding salaries and rent, each book costs about 94c. That's less than €30 per class group.

The model is very similar to that used in 826 Valencia in San Francisco, and the other 826 centres throughout the USA. In 2004, I was in San Francisco, promoting a new book. My friend, Dave Eggers, asked me to come down to his relatively new writing centre, 826 Valencia. (The name is the street number, 826, on Valencia Street.) I found the place easily enough. The building itself was nondescript but beautifully decorated. There was a shop mannequin, a boy, dressed in early twentieth-century clothes, his back to the window. He was looking at San Francisco, a black-and-white photo that ran the length of the window. I stepped into the shop; it *is* a shop – a store. It sells pirate accessories – peg legs, eye patches, doubloons, hats. It was dark, like the inside of an old ship. I could hear children's voices behind a black curtain. I eventually found a way through it, and saw a version of what I've just described, a group of children writing a story. I sat at the back and watched. It was the most magical experience. It was so simple, straightforward and yet it seemed newly invented, a surprise. It worked on so many levels, including theatrical. It was the planning and the performance. It seemed natural, *and* still feels natural, to clap when it was over.

I was back in San Francisco two years later and this time I stayed longer. I went out with 826 volunteers, to see what they did with high school children. An old secondary teacher myself, I found this even more exciting than the work being done with the little kids. It's almost impossible not to love a six-year-old; it's much more difficult to find the charm in someone else's sixteen-year-old. I took notes, I asked questions: What worked well? What went wrong? I filled a notebook and came home. I knew I needed a partner, an executive director. Seán Love was at that time CEO of Amnesty Ireland. We'd known each other for five or six years; I'd done some writing and educational work for Amnesty. Almost immediately, we started walking Dublin's inner city, looking for possible premises. The name, Fighting Words, came quickly. There was a blank space on our Charitable Status application form, so we put in 'Fighting Words' – for the time being. And it stuck. People loved it, and so did we. We've been open since January 2009 and more than 40,000 primary and secondary students, and older people, many of whom seem to have been bypassed by the education system, have been through the magic door.

About three weeks after we opened, a group of young women came to us. They were taking part in a back to work scheme; they were all early school leavers. They wanted to write a story, they said, but they didn't know how. They had a plan – four friends in their early 20s, living at home in their different houses; the excitement of their lives, and the difficulties; alcoholic parents, absent parents, grandmother with Alzheimer's, depression, unemployment. They wanted it to be funny but real. But they didn't know how to go about it.

In the few weeks we'd been open we'd seen the impact of the screen, the excitement it created, the fun and, in many cases, the temporary removal of the fear and anxiety that the physical act of writing can awaken or reawaken. It had worked with young children. We wondered if we could use it with teenagers and older people. So we asked two of the young women, Hayley and Emer, to imagine themselves as two of the characters, and to talk – just talk – to each other. They didn't want to stand, so they sat with their friends in front of the screen and they started to talk. A typist tried to keep up with them. They were funny, and quickly began to enjoy themselves. After a minute or so, they stopped, and read what had gone up on the screen as they'd talked. They loved it.

'It's like real talking,' said Hayley.

They loved that, the fact that their spoken words were good enough to go up on a screen, or page. Almost immediately, they began to edit what was there.

'I don't like that,' said Hayley.

She stood up and walked over to the screen and pointed at a line of dialogue.

'I wouldn't say that,' she said.

We laughed. So did she.

'You *did* fuckin' say that,' said one of her friends.

But Hayley was right. She'd decided that they could come up with something better. It didn't matter what had actually been said; fiction could be an improvement.

By the end of the first hour, the girls had added detail to the dialogue, and they'd decided to write in the present tense. Here's the first page:

> It is July, the month Janice is about to turn 18, and the girls are at the local Eurospar, discussing plans and what to do for the occasion. Leanne suggests a meal with the four of them, while Donna wants something more lively, like a night out on the town. Jessica suggests the girls discuss this with Janice's family to see if they have any plans made already.
>
> They all leave and head home. Later that evening Leanne gets a phone call from Jessica. She tells her that Janice's ma rang her and said she's organizing a surprise 18th birthday party for Janice.
>
> Leanne is chuffed. 'Another big night out for the girls,' she thinks. Leanne hangs up the phone and calls Donna.

Donna answers, 'Hello?'

'Heya, what's up?' Leanne says.

'Aw, you sound happy,' Donna replies.

'Guess what? Jan's ma is throwin' her a surprise party.'

'No way, where's she havin' it?'

'Ah, don't know yet,' says Leanne. 'Probably The Club House.'

'Lovely stuff. Have to get somethin' nice to wear. Will we book a limo?'

'Ah, yeah. Right Donna, I have to go. There's a knock at the door.'

'Okay, g'wan. Bye.'

The women had started a novel. They loved seeing a phrase of their own, 'lovely stuff', being spoken by a fictional character. They loved deciding to spell 'go on' as they wanted it heard, 'g'wan'. They loved choosing the names for their characters. They laughed when they decided to put the girls outside the local Eurospar.

They came to us regularly for a couple of months. If we'd asked them, when they'd first arrived, to sit at the tables and write, we wouldn't have seen them again. The screen, and the handing over of some of the more worrying, crippling parts of the process – spelling, punctuation – and the sight of their own words going up there, the simplicity of it – allowed them to get straight to the core of the thing, the story and the words that make the story.

Writing is a solitary occupation – eventually. But I've witnessed it again and again: if the writing starts as a collective exercise, a bit of fun, almost a piece of theatre, by the time the young writers go to the tables and start to write by themselves, they produce better, more confident work. They've seen what they can do, the simple things that can make a good line brilliant, and they're keen to give it a go themselves.

So the screen has become our weapon of choice. We always start with it – a small piece of role play. We have different situations for different groups, depending on age and gender. We keep it simple: two characters.

Two girls talking, one of whom fancies the other's brother; this always works with young women of fifteen and older. The girl with the brother, with the bit of power, invariably and immediately becomes a complete wagon. The results on the screen are often hilarious, sometimes explosive, a great start and a great invitation to continue.

Two friends, one of whom has just won two tickets for a gig, the other assuming he or she is getting it, but isn't; this one always works. I witnessed one unforgettable session when two fifteen-year-old boys became the two friends and, inside a minute, one of them, the lad with the tickets and the power, shouted at the other: 'You stole my girlfriend.' A great line, and they knew it. Everyone knew it – after we'd stopped laughing and applauding. They couldn't wait to get to the tables, to start their own versions, to get their own characters to that line, and past it.

Two friends outside the principal's office; one of them has broken a window and has accused the other of aiding and abetting. This one works with younger boys – and girls. The dialogue goes up, then questions like, 'Why are they there?' 'Where was the window?' 'What are their names?' 'How long do they wait?' 'Will we let them talk a bit first, then explain why they're there?' 'Where will we put that?' produce answers and ideas, and contradictions that have to be dealt with, and better ideas, the deletion of lines, the insertion of other lines. Writing, in other words.

Obviously, the real work – the writer's future – starts at the tables, when the decisions become personal and difficult. Even the brightest kids are often terrified. So we start at the screen, then move away. 'What can be done', before 'what can't be done.'

Write first, worry later.

On theft: teaching poetry composition to undergraduates

SINÉAD MORRISSEY

WHAT DO I TEACH AND WHO DO I TEACH?

Just before his death, in a letter to Adrienne Rich, the great American poet Randall Jarrell asserted: 'To have written one good poem – *good* used seriously – is an unlikely and marvellous thing that only a couple of hundred writers of English, at the most, have done'[1] My own list of poets in English who have written 'one good poem' is much longer than that of Jarrell: I am perpetually grateful to the many brilliant poets in English, from Ireland, the UK, the US, from Canada, New Zealand and Australia, to poets living and to poets dead, who inspire me to do better. There is no dearth of them, and I couldn't continue to write without them.

It is nevertheless true that a good poem is 'a marvellous thing', dependent not only on craftsmanship and a sound intellect, but on a kind of magic, a linguistic alchemy that transmutes the words used into something more than themselves. If a good poem is 'unlikely' (and I agree with Jarrell that it is), how can you teach people to write one? Perhaps even more outlandish a proposal is the idea that you can teach fifteen Stage Two students who are taking a module in Creative Writing as part of a general undergraduate literature degree to do it over the course of a single semester. And not only to do it once, but to do it fifteen times, as they assemble their final portfolio, which in turn is marked according to set criteria – the price tag attached to bringing poetry composition as a viable subject into the academy.

It is not possible to teach talent. Nor is it possible to teach or control the alchemical side of the process (which many call inspiration). Nor, most obviously, is it possible to teach intelligence, the 'sound intellect', a requirement of the 'good' poet. But it is possible to teach *equally important* things: the basics of poetic craft (lineation,

---

[1] Cited in Dennis O'Driscoll, *Troubled thoughts, majestic dreams* (Loughcrew, 2001), p. 61.

structure, form); the (ideally) dynamic relationship between form and content; the rules of successful poetic language. In her introduction to *52 ways of looking at a poem,* Ruth Padel distils these rules down to three essential principles: showing not telling, specificity, and economy.[2] As a teacher and a poet, I return to these principles constantly. These three rules steer writers away from all sorts of follies: hectoring, rhetoric, verbosity, self-absorption. If they're at the heart of a Creative Writing poetry module, alongside the basics of poetic craft and an awareness of the form/content relationship, what you can offer students is a sort of invaluable short-cut: years of solitary reading and thinking condensed into a twelve-week package.

Which is not to say such principles will be grasped – much less mastered – in that time. For many writing is, and should remain, a long road. But through such an intensive course of reading and writing poetry, now on offer in many universities, the enterprise of writing 'good' poems can be made clearer, the formal and linguistic skill of 'good' poems be more keenly understood, and, most ambitiously, the structures and rules of poetry become connected in students' minds to other artistic phenomena in the wider world: music, the visual arts, architecture. This is how I set out my stall in course descriptions and at the beginning of a module. Who, then, are my students and what are they looking for?

Every year, I teach at least one student at undergraduate level who is stunningly good; in some years there are as many as four or five of them. Such students have the necessary ingredients that cannot be taught: intelligence and talent. Provide them with a formal grounding, the rules of the craft in shorthand, and they invariably excel. After a certain point, such students are clearly unteachable, if only because what I know becomes superfluous to their needs. Some have gone on to publish; others, though writing poetry of a higher quality than much of what *is* published, have not, or have not published yet.

At the other end of the scale are very poor students, who view Creative Writing as an easy option because it doesn't ostensibly involve a long reading list of eighteenth-century novels. These students neither read poetry nor care about it and generally do not improve. Such students are also, thankfully, in the minority.

2 Ruth Padel, *52 ways of looking at a poem, or, how reading modern poetry can change your life* (London, 2002), p. 9.

To the majority of students a Creative Writing poetry module is one module out of many, and not a *wildly* exciting opportunity at that. These students are genuinely interested in poetry (though they may not be all that widely read, particularly in the field of contemporary poetry) and they enjoy the weekly writing tasks, which they take seriously. They will probably never be published poets and they don't hold any publishing or long-term poetry aspirations, though their work undoubtedly improves over the course of the module, and they become more adept readers of their own and others' work.

As well as teaching these students why it isn't a good idea (in most instances) to overload a poem with adjectives and adverbs, the course repeatedly teaches them awareness of the articulacy of form – of the effects of their decisions (to use a long line or a short line, to use stanzas or to write in a single block of text, to use or to forgo punctuation). Having tried one themselves, they will probably never read a sestina without an intimate appreciation of its workings again. Basic grammatical considerations are taken in along the way: that a comma does not function in a sentence in the same way as a full-stop; that a sentence must be comprised of a subject and a verb (at least); and that some verbs require an object and some do not. Such students experience the satisfaction, which cannot be overestimated, of being in charge of making something themselves, rather than interpreting something by somebody else, and if they work hard, are prepared to edit their poems in the light of feedback, and have the sense to meaningfully title and order their final portfolio, they can do moderately well, or at least as well as on other academic courses.

Because the teachable part of poetry is to do with aspects of craft, and because the majority of my students at this stage require structure and direction, my own undergraduate Creative Writing poetry module is based around a series of micro-topics, which include three set forms (the sonnet, the villanelle and the sestina), rhythm, imagery, concrete poetry and Ekphrasis. For the rest of this essay, I'd like to concentrate on two interconnected micro-topics that I use at the beginning of the course: the found poem, and imitation. Both are varieties of theft: found poetry steals the language from somewhere else and organizes it into an appropriate poetic form; imitation poetry steals the formal template from another poem, and fills it with different language. Together, they can teach students some of the fundamental principles of successful poetic structure and content while providing them, in each instance, with half the work already done. The latter part of the course is more open-ended, when students are freer to choose what they want to say and how they want to say it. At the beginning, by contrast, these two exercises are designed to help students to walk before they can run.

THE FOUND POEM

In 1917, the Dadaist Marcel Duchamp famously caused uproar among artistic circles by renaming a urinal 'Fountain' and claiming it as a new, artistic work. The urinal was signed (though not by him), and apart from looking wrenched off the wall of a public toilet, and therefore ceasing to function according to its original intention, it had otherwise remained unchanged. That the urinal was not altered, but that its context was changed, and therefore its intention and function, is relevant to the definition of the found poem.

In his collection *Ice Age,* Paul Farley includes a found poem, 'Relic':

> One's a crown, two's a crown,
> Three, four, five distal occlusion,
> Six distal occlusion, seven occlusal.
> Upper left: one mesial incisal,
> Two mesial incisal, three's a crown,
> Four, five is absent, space closed.
> Six occlusal, seven occlusal, eight.
> Lower left: one's a crown, two mesial,
> Three, four occlusal, five is absent,
> Space closed. Six occlusal, seven occlusal,
> Eight is absent. Right: one, two, three,
> Four distant occlusal, five's a buckle,
> Six and seven are absent, space closed.[3]

'Relic' is comprised entirely of a dentist's initial examination of his teeth, which Farley recorded and then transcribed as above. But found poems can be made up of *any* language which the poet does not write

---

3 Paul Farley, 'Relic' in *The ice age* (London, 2002), p. 35.

him/herself. This language can be taken from anywhere: letters, newspaper articles, contents pages, scientific dictionaries, technology manuals, gardening guides. To go looking to *find* a poem means having your eyes and ears open to the rich, distinctive lexica and cadences of all sorts of language, both written and overheard, as it is manifested in the wider world. The language you find as the raw material for your poem must be interesting and resonant with multiple possible meanings. To ask students to go forth and find such language is to test, and hopefully refresh, their ideas of what constitutes poetic language in the first place.

It is important that the original author's intentions for the language were *not* poetic. To take Chapter One of *Genesis* in the St James' Authorized Version of the Bible and to break it into lines (as I have had at least one student do) will not work as a found poem because the text is already poetry. To rearrange pop lyrics, lyrical prose or worst of all, other poems, will fall flat. The surprise and pleasure of a successful found poem lie, as with Duchamp's urinal, in the switching of the original language's *context*, and hence in the transformation of *meaning* which inevitably follows. To take the letter of a nineteenth-century slave owner offering a reward for a runaway slave, and to turn this into a poem by a contemporary American poet, without commentary, thereby transforming the intention of the original language completely, is an example of how politically charged the found poem can be.[4] One of my best students took an article by an American reporter, who was a supporter of capital punishment, on the difficulty of getting to attend all the executions currently taking place in the State of Texas. She turned his pro-death penalty stance on its head, by doing nothing other than re-casting his article as a poem and thereby infusing the whole with irony.

To ask students to 'write' a found poem is not only to test their awareness of the inherently poetic possibilities of unexpected language. After you've found your source, the real work of the found poem lies in its construction. A suitable container for this language must be fashioned, and here students will engage with basic structural aspects of writing any poem: what kind of line to use, where to break the lines,

---

4 Kevin Young, 'Reward' in H.L. Hix (ed.), *New voices: contemporary poetry from the United States* (Belfast, 2008), pp 137–8.

whether to use stanzas, how many lines should each stanza contain, and so on. In each instance, they should be able to justify their choice. In Paul Farley's 'Relic', the text is squashed together, for example, without the white space of a stanza break (or breaks). This compression formally mirrors the repetition of 'space closed'. Additionally, he has made the by now unusual decision to automatically capitalize the first letter of each line. An effect of this is to augment the formal, cold tone of the poem. The title 'Relic' fuses undergoing a dental examination with the identification of the dead via dental records: the whole poem is deliberately, and brilliantly, impersonal, and its five distinct absences, which refer to extracted teeth, come to resonate with the absence of anything else by which a human body might be reliably identified.

IMITATION

It is unlikely that anyone will write a good poem without being a good reader of poetry. We write in conversation with other poems, with other poetic models which help us to find our way through a difficulty, or which offer an alternative perspective on our current obsession. Translations, versions, the words '*after* [name of a poet]' after a title – all of these testify to the ongoing and robust dialogue which poets pursue with poems other than their own. Carol Ann Duffy's anthology from 2008, *Answering back,* in which she asked fifty poets to 'take on' an older poem in a poem of their own,[5] was a welcome commission for many of the poets who responded to their chosen addressees with wit and passion.

The majority of the poems in this anthology leave the structure of the original poem behind: some look very different; some look similar but are not exactly the same; few mirror the original's line-length, number of lines, stanzaic shape and number of stanzas precisely (not to mention rhyme scheme, if there is one). Again, because my own imitation exercise comes at the beginning of a beginner's course, and because rules are more helpful at this stage than a lack of them, I ask my students to mirror the form of their chosen poems *as closely as they can manage to*. Ideally, I want the formal mirroring to be exact. In the found

---

5 Carol Ann Duffy (ed.), *Answering back: living poets reply to the poetry of the past* (London, 2008).

poem exercise, students build a poem to correspond to pre-given language; here they must fill in a borrowed formal template with their own language, like filling a jar with just the right liquid. It is an opposite, but complementary, undertaking.

As with found poetry, there are more and less successful ways of going about the imitation exercise. There are (at least) two ways in which an Ekphrastic poem (or a poem responding to a visual artifact) can fail: if the poem is not sufficiently connected to the painting it is inspired by, or if it is *too* connected – if the poem simply describes what is already there in the painting. Similarly with imitation, there *must* be a solid connection to the original, both in terms of form *and* content. But there must also be a twist. Straightforward eulogizing, or agreeing with the sentiment of the first poem, is boring. One would ask what the impetus behind bothering to write the second poem might be. Possibilities for the nature of the twist are thankfully endless: a direct and angry counter-address; an unexpected voice or point of view; a bathetic switch in activity; a different time or context. Alan Gillis is a contemporary Irish poet particularly adept at the urban update, for example – at taking a pre-existing poem set in a sentimentalized countryside and placing it in a vibrant, drug-ridden, alcoholic, violent, bang-up-to-the-minute milieu. The joke wouldn't be successful if we didn't recognize the original poem behind the new work, but the real thrust and verve of the joke lie in the shift in context and vocabulary itself. His work is fresh, dazzlingly energetic and formally impressive – often a model for what the directly imitative poem can achieve.

Similarly, R.S. Gwynn has produced a hilarious re-working of Philip Larkin's 'Mr Bleaney': 'Mr Heaney'. Even the similarity of surname and title is funny. In 'Mr Heaney', the speaker, as in Larkin's original poem, is shown into a room formally occupied by the eponymous subject of the poem. As in the original, the speaker of 'Mr Heaney' looks out the window at a dismal scene ('And so it is I lie where Heaney lay/And watch the twilight dripping with the murk/Lurking beyond short curtains'), and muses on the life lived out in the room before him. He concludes:

> Such cause for wonderment. Did Heaney ask
> No better than a spade or pen or hoe

> To kill his time? Nothing to ease the task –
> Girls, say? Or hurling pools? I just don't know.[6]

The formal structure of the original, including rhyme scheme, is precisely mirrored, and the double thrust of the poem, which manages to (gently) satirize both Philip Larkin and Seamus Heaney, beautifully controlled.

I'm considering banning 'This be the Verse' by Philip Larkin for the imitation exercise, and not only because too many students use it (sometimes I despair that this is the only contemporary poem students *like*), but also because students often cannot bring themselves to change the awful sentiment of the original enough. They seem to feel viscerally that Larkin was right. That said, the range of original poems used can be gratifyingly surprising: work by Simon Armitage, Constantine Cavafy, Alfred Tennyson, Carol Ann Duffy, Thomas Hardy, Michael Longley, Anna Akhmatava and Ciaran Carson, has all been used without prompting by me. The very best students not only pay sufficient attention to the structure of the original and demonstrate formal control; they also write suitably inflected content. The most memorable imitation poem by a student took Longley's elegy for an assassinated ice-cream man and used its unforgettable list of flavours as a vehicle to mourn a fellow secondary-school student (who was brilliant at maths) via a list of mathematical terms and instruments.

RULES VERSUS FREEDOM

As a whole, my undergraduate introductory module on poetry composition functions rather like a set poetic form: just as there are rules to a villanelle (and if you break them, you just don't have a villanelle anymore), there are things on the course each week with which the students *have* to engage. With the three set forms themselves, there is little room for deviation, but equally the students must undertake the other writing exercises (including the found poem and imitation) with set guidelines in mind. The course advocates, by implication, a model of poetry composition which is grounded in technique. A poem

---

6 R.S. Gwynn, 'Mr Heaney' in Rory Waterman and Nick Everett (eds), *New walk*, 5, (Autumn/Winter 2012–13), 9.

becomes a challenge or a problem to be solved with as much ingenuity and *élan* as possible. It is a far cry from the Romantic notion of inspiration and advocates an idea of poetic composition as a craftperson's endeavour, for which there are multiple, special-purpose tools and which requires practice – self-editing and working through drafts in terms of the individual poem, and more generally, years of work, of getting it wrong, of experimenting, of pushing oneself beyond comfort zones, of daring to fail. This work happens in the midst of, and as a result of, a dynamic conversation with other poets, and can last a lifetime.

What, then, of content? Content I generally leave up to the students, believing (probably naively) that there are no taboo subjects, just better or less successful means of articulation (though navel-gazing and heartfelt expressions of misery are prevented, or to some extent limited, by a ban on abstract nouns). In an attempt to get students to focus less on their own interior world of subjective emotion and to look more cleanly on the world about them, and to render that exterior reality in fresh language, the haiku has proved inordinately useful, with its grounding in the senses, on what is observed, or heard, and in its Zen-like absence of an I. The maxim 'write about what you know' is a tricky one. On the one hand I encourage students to write about what they *don't* know – to go beyond their usual subject matter, to take on another voice – and via writing to arrive at a new knowledge. But sometimes what they already know (setting aside getting drunk a lot and being late for class) is unexpected enough to be a great source of poetry. One student's final portfolio based entirely around his boxing club, and the gruelling mornings spent jogging in Belfast rain – experiences rooted in the student's lived experience – was very striking.

Teaching poetry composition at MA- or PhD-level is very different. Here you have a group of self-selecting, highly motivated students who passionately want to write. Many of them, especially the mature students, have been writing for years. The assumption behind my teaching at this level is that the fundamentals of poetic craft are already known, and the teaching is more open-ended – responding, in workshops, to what the students are undertaking themselves, guiding class discussion (which is often at a sophisticated level) and introducing students to the work of other poets which might be relevant to their own practice. Supplementary modules to the workshop are designed to challenge students to write in unfamiliar ways: to undertake research and to use it for a new sequence; to engage with differing models of structuring a poetry collection; to try their hand at translation.

Ideally, the aim behind the two approaches – more structured at undergraduate level, more open-ended at postgraduate level – is to teach students to fly, and then watch them take off. Which actually happens often enough to make my job a privilege, rather than a necessity.

Beginnings: becoming a teacher of creative writing

LEANNE O'SULLIVAN

Last summer it had been more than eight months since I had written a poem. It had been months since I had a spark of an idea, or that 'lump in the throat, a sense of wrong, a homesickness, a lovesickness' that Frost describes – 'a reaching out towards expression'.[1] I had finished a book of poems during the previous winter, sent it off to my publisher and felt delighted with a job done, as well as I could have done it. I was looking forward to teaching and reading and a slowing down of the days, since nothing makes a day disappear more than when I am trying to write a poem. I had spent over four years thinking about and writing these poems and they had become my work, what I would work at, make. In the absence then of a project I began to grope around for the odd bit of poetry, a hangover of a line I didn't use, a poem that at one stage might not have seemed worth marking the page for. However, my efforts began without the niggling, necessary 'lump in the throat'. Although I am beginning to respect my own pattern with writing and have come to learn that, like the seasons, there is a time when poetry goes underground and re-spools itself, I cannot help nursing the anxiety that I will not write another poem that I like. I also suspect that in my case, as a young writer, poetry will sometimes go underground and emerge differently, looking a few inches taller and walking a bit straighter (one hopes). I believe in the apprenticeship of the craft and have chosen, in this essay, to approach the question of Creative Writing workshops not only as someone who has led classes as a teacher/facilitator/guide, but also as student who can bear witness to the value and complexities of these experiences.

It had been quite a few years since I had taken a Creative Writing workshop, having timorously stepped into the role of leading and facilitating classes instead. Over the years I had decided that my greatest teachers were not only the ones I had taken workshops with in the past,

---

[1] Letter to Louis Untermeyer, 1 January 1916. See Louis Untermeyer (ed.), *The letters of Robert Frost to Louis Untermeyer* (London, 1963), p. 22.

but also the ones on my bookshelves – Eavan Boland, Paula Meehan, Seamus Heaney, Michael Longley, Ruth Stone, among many others – and I had never taken workshops with them. Whatever the mystery which propels a poem, it doesn't ever emerge in isolation. Poetry, and indeed music and conversation, stir, teach and train the listening consciousness. All the possibilities for rhythm, cadence, line-endings, pause, punctuation, form, experiment, beginnings, endings, bravery, and even silence have stirred me through the work of other artists and have helped me shape my own poems, not least because of the pleasure I take from reading other poems. What poetry lover does not dream of making their own mark? However, last summer I believed I needed something more collegial than the books on my bookshelves. I had felt myself turning a corner in my writing, and although I hadn't yet found myself in the middle of a dark wood, I had begun questioning my endeavour as a writer. Painters, sculptors and carpenters have all traditionally had to attend workshops to share ideas, tools, innovations and camaraderie, so it is not surprising that writers, on such a solitary path, would also want to meet for these reasons. With the understanding that I am still an apprentice myself, and on finding myself at a crossroads, I decided to take a poetry workshop.

The workshop I chose was being taught by a poet whom I had only just discovered for myself a few months before, and whose work had become a touchstone for me. I signed up and nervously took my place with the other participants. I say nervously because I was never a good student – in the academic classroom or the creative one – and would dread assignments and in-class exercises. I would be struck by stage-fright, even in the privacy of my own house, when I would try to turn out some kind of verse to be 'workshopped' the following day. More often than not, I would dig out something I had begun months ago – something in bad enough shape but not hopeless – to read in the class when my turn came around. In my hiatus between taking workshops as a teenager and taking them as an adult writer I have begun to realize and accept that I write rarely and slowly, preferring a long, 'listening' curiosity about the poem I might someday write. What then did I expect from this week-long workshop?

Creative Writing workshops assist new and seasoned writers in a number of ways, not least of all in providing an atmosphere where a writer feels supported, but also where he/she becomes confident enough to take risks. It is important to remember that most writers are beginners, or at least feel that they are, since every poem is a new undertaking with its own puzzle of crossroads – and indeed cross words. When we offer our work to be discussed, particularly in a workshop or writing group when it's not entirely finished, we are exposing a vulnerable part of ourselves. We invest some of our self-esteem in our writing and hope that our critics will be sensitive in their responses. However, if a poem is not constructively challenged then a workshop is not doing its work. By encouraging a sympathetic atmosphere, keeping in mind the poet as 'maker' and the value we place in poetry, participants will be more encouraged to roll up their sleeves. The job of the workshop leader – the writer at the head of the table – is to organize ways in which these students might develop in some direction their own relationship with their writing. Prompts and exercises are a wonderful and useful way to break the ice, and if a writer is open to this spontaneity something else might happen – accident, luck, perception, excitement, a way in.

Although I feel that I am just beginning my poetic or literary apprenticeship, my earliest experience of writing poetry began when I was about twelve years old. I'm from a very rural part of Ireland and we lived about two-and-a-half hours from Cork city, on the Beara Peninsula. In the mid-nineties the resources meant to encourage young people to write and be creative, in writers' centres, writers' retreats libraries and so on, were few and very far between and it was difficult and expensive for our school to make them available. In spite of that, however, my lasting and most lively memories of secondary school all revolve around the discovery, reading and making of poetry. When I started secondary school at the age of twelve my English teacher arranged for the Co. Waterford poet, Thomas McCarthy, to visit our school to give a two-day writing workshop. All of the first- and second-year students were told that if any of us could show that we had some interest in writing or in poetry we could have the two days off from our usual afternoon classes to take part in Tom's workshop. This was my first exercise, or prompt, to write poetry. It was driven purely by my dislike of whatever classes I would be missing, but also the incentive of doing something different. So that particular evening after school twenty or so children began to write poetry in earnest. Taking advantage of not having completely forgotten the airs and graces of the nursery rhyme, we filled pages with sonnets, ballads and limericks – to prove ourselves worthy to take part. The point was not to be good, but to begin.

People take workshops for all kinds of reasons. Some come with a manuscript of poems that spans many years of their writing lives and are eager to have it discussed and made presentable for publication; some want to know how to make their poems more effective. Others come to truly begin, having never attempted a poem before, to re-create in verse some aspect of their experience and are looking for support. Some might come to listen, and may have no intention of ever writing a poem. It is highly probable that a classroom will have all of these people waiting, excitedly and anxiously, to begin. Indeed anxiety and excitement are two sides of the same coin when it comes to Creative Writing. Young or new writers look up to published and older poets and wonder how we can beat our own paths. When I begin to feel that lump in my throat I wonder if I am up to the challenge and often think about the contest with the bow in *The Odyssey*, with the suitors watching how swiftly Odysseus can string the instrument and, before he even lets go the arrow to hit the mark, he plucks the string of the bow to make it sing. We imagine the writers we love writing just as swiftly, just as freely, and even though we know this notion is only fancy we wonder how we can do it too. It was only when I sat down to take my first workshop in almost a decade that I realized how full of anxiety I had become – how some new beginning had unnerved me and I wondered how would I proceed, how would I write. Would the poems be poems? Would they be my poems? I don't believe in writer's block, but anxiety is the wolf that keeps the poems from the door.

An experience I had as a workshop leader for a group of beginners (around the same time I took this summer workshop) was in a classroom in Dublin where approximately fifteen adults signed up for the class. It was a one-off, one-day workshop which would focus on the use of voice and poetic persona in poetry. Since we were meeting for such a short amount of time and the room was slightly pitched with uncertainties it took a while to settle in and allow people to relax. I was well underway in discussing my topic when a gentleman at the opposite side of the table raised his hand to ask a question – a fairly standard question – what was my writing process like? Although the class had been advertised as focusing on voice/persona it soon became clear to me that the participants that day were each looking for some kind of encouragement or reassurance, and could take or leave my spiel on persona. I replied that I wrote rarely and slowly and that I would normally write eight or ten poems in a year, preferring to think them through over a long period of time – after which you could have heard a pin drop on the carpet. For a moment I wondered if I should indeed be writing more poems, if there was something faulty in my process, but after a few more questions about quantity, length, the work of getting poems written, the trial and error, I found my footing on this subject and the workshop continued in a much more relaxed way. I also quoted from Michael Longley's poem, 'Once':

> You only have to do it once,
> Write a poem, I mean, one poem
> As good as the elegy
> For himself that Chidiock
> Tichborne jotted down
> The night before the gallows,
> Castration, disembowelment,
> A smile on his face, surely,
> As he found the syllables
> And the breathing spaces.[2]

I wonder now, in thinking about my own experiences as a student, if what I did in that Dublin workshop was simply de-mystify the notion of prolific poetic inspiration; of the full-time poet writing easefully into the dawn with the muse sitting on her shoulder. I wonder if I had said something true about the effort needed to make a poem – there is the first ache in the throat, but what comes after that (in my case) is a patient nudging, then images, then words, fallibility, chance, the line, sound, music, and shape/form. There is a great deal of work and 'dear labour', and also the fear that the initial inspiration for the poem won't hold water. How wonderful to know this about writers and poets, and how else would we have these conversations without the concentrated space a workshop provides, 'the breathing spaces'.

This is especially important to remember when teaching young

2 Michael Longley, 'Once' in *A hundred doors* (London, 2011), p. 50.

people and I am reminded once again of that first workshop with Thomas McCarthy. At the time we were studying poets who were no longer alive or would never meet. As yet we had no idea of the living and steady poetic tradition in Ireland. I had not thought that poetry could be relevant to my life – to our lives as young people, at the time very young people. I didn't believe that poetry had anything to do with me, although I found solace and a kind of emotional map in music and song. I felt that I could experience music – that the rhythms of song could become a part of me and move me – yet I had felt excluded by the discourse of poetic expression as taught in school. As young people we were enjoying poetry without reading it; for example I believe the lyrics of U2 could stand up to many published poems. But the way poetry was taught in school never made a connection with these obvious points of access. Poetry was always seen as something in a museum, something inert, dusty and locked in a cabinet, hermetically sealed. Because of his encouragement and ability to lift ourselves and poetry onto the same playing field, what happened in those two days with Tom McCarthy became a grounding for me in the rest of my school days, and indeed right into today. I say playing field because that is how it began for me – a shy playfulness with words and phrases, and a gathering of language and forms I used until I felt confident enough to construct my own. Meeting a poet who wrote about an Ireland I could see, hear, and inhabit eased much of the anxiety I had felt about writing. Perhaps I could write poetry. Perhaps I could make that choice.

I also believe that as we came to know poetry more we found it difficult to escape a shyness or hesitancy in dealing with a form that we still found distant and difficult – a nervousness of the unknown and the nakedness of expression that would come before any craftwork would be done. It is only now after having taught Creative Writing to young people over the last few years that I realize while poetry is seen as a sophisticated and developed form of discourse it is also something that is deeply primitive. I mean the term 'primitive' in a positive sense. It is one of the first instincts of our species to make a poem or song. The earliest writings in communities and languages are invariably poetic, such as *Beowulf* and the *Epic of Gilgamesh*. As we know, the word 'poet' itself simply means 'a maker', and in the absence of any other tools to make sense of the world writing or reciting is one of the most available forms of expression, especially to young people. Just as early societies made their first utterances in poetic forms so too analogously should young people find in poetry a natural form for expressing their own burgeoning sense of identity and place. This is what I meant by primitive. And while a certain amount of shyness or hesitation can be there initially, I've found in the case of the young people I've worked with that the balance generally shifts to a sphere in which there is less inhibition, where they can feel more confident in their voices and in their opinions, passions and thoughts.

To cite another example from my own teaching experience, a couple of years ago I was invited by a cultural centre in England to facilitate a poetry workshop for a group of fourteen-year-olds from economically disadvantaged backgrounds in a formally industrialized British inner city. There were about twelve students there – some had been abandoned by their parents and were already homeless in the world – some were being severely bullied in school, others were the bullies. It was particularly nerve-wracking for me, as I began to wonder what could I teach these potentially hardened and hurt children about poetry? Looking back on it now I see it was one of the best teaching experiences for me yet. By the beginning of the second day there was an energizing sense of camaraderie among the students, as if they had just met each other, and were determined suddenly to work together, to encourage each other, with honesty and courtesy, to write. By mid-week I really did feel like a teacher who had faded back into the walls, watching the children take flight as they became more confident and determined. I remember one of the students who was particularly difficult to get through to, who had suffered extreme trauma in her home context and at school, and who had such a protective shell around her it seemed at the beginning that nothing was getting in and nothing was coming out. She repeated over and over again that she could not write poetry. However, over the course of the week she gradually allowed herself to peer over her insecurity and began to think about and experiment with poetry. She started to project outwards onto the page her sense of herself and at the same time to register more subtly the people to whom she related and the context around her.

And of course this is not all a poetry workshop can do. The confidence builds slowly and what sustains it is learning how to employ some tools of the craft. There is no way a teacher or writer can tell us how to write a good poem. It is a highly individual and creative act, and most writers agree that the making of a poem involves some kind of mystery. If the mystery could be taught, poetry would die. So what might happen in a workshop besides the ... inspiration, encouragement? This is where we can begin to refine the effectiveness of how we communicate our subject or idea through attention to what we might call poetic craft – which is the ever increasing self-awareness we bring to the choices we make and that has to be in balance (or in tension) with the inner voice of poetry we have and cannot seem to control. We learn to become aware of word choice, sound, imagery, the line, the possibilities of form. Through reading and discussion the initial drafts or raw material can begin to resemble and sound like a poem. We can explore specific techniques and forms and ways of expression. Most importantly, however, we can gently build that crucial awareness while at the same time protecting our own unique process. Exercises are wonderful if we can use them appropriately – whether focusing on honing a particular aspect of poetry such as working with forms, metaphor, imagery, or simply lightly and playfully nudging the student on towards making a mark rather than hitting one.

Although I sometimes use exercises in my own workshops, I was overjoyed when my teacher last summer decided not to inflict such hard work on us! It was very easy and relaxed with wonderful conversations about poetry, favourite poems, and it was, above all else, a sustained and constructive response to work we had already brought in. Taking the class also made me realize that this is what most students especially value, in particular the ones who have been writing quietly for some time – affirmation and the opportunity to think of themselves as writers, for the duration of the course at least. What follows is sustaining the writing practice in our own solitude, buoyed by the encouragement we received directly or indirectly from the workshop group. We also learn certain skills, and most importantly to look at each blank page as a chance to learn through our own trial and error. We learn that there is a certain mystery to writing poetry, also that clearing away fears is as conducive to writing as any craftwork. As a student I felt I also got what I needed from my summer hiatus, which was to listen to a poet talk about his life with poetry, and I reached the end of the week with far fewer anxieties and much more trust.

Imaginative constellations: the creative writing workshop as laboratory

PAUL PERRY

> To begin to write – to attempt anything creative, for that matter – is to ask many questions, not only about the craft itself, but of oneself, and of life.[1]

With Hanif Kureishi's pronouncement in mind, this essay, and the writing experiment that accompanies it, is an attempt to redress the neglected questions about 'oneself', which are wrapped up in the endeavour to write at all.

Creative Writing has been reduced almost exclusively to the workshop method argues D.G. Myers.[2] The use of the word 'reduced' gives this assertion a rather derogatory inflection. The implication is that students no longer read anything other than their peers' own creative efforts, and that Creative Writing exists in a critical vacuum of its own making. Teachers of Creative Writing know this is not true. We teach literature courses, literary history, theory, reading as a writer, and very often students can opt to take elective courses outside of the English or Creative Writing department to amplify their own research interests, whether they are in the areas of anthropology, psychology, music or media studies.

The vast variation on what is offered in Creative Writing programmes and how it is delivered refutes Myers' contention. And yet there is something insistent in his argument. One of the solutions to what may manifest itself beyond the workshop, Myers posits, is what Paul Dawson recommends, which is to transform Creative Writing into 'a discipline of knowledge' and discard the Creative Writing ethos of free expression and replace it with a 'sociological poetics'.[3]

That Creative Writing should take on a social purpose sounds rather didactic to me. This would involve a relegation of the workshop as

---

[1] Hanif Kureishi, *Collected essays* (London, 2011), p. 282. [2] D.G. Myers, *The elephants teach: creative writing since 1800* (Chicago, 2006), p. 175. [3] Quoted in ibid., p. 8 and p. 9.

something central to Creative Writing pedagogy. Rather than a relegation or dismissal of the workshop in Creative Writing pedagogy, I believe, the workshop, as an evolving tool or arena, can be looked at as a model in flux, an ever-changing, protean space of learning in Creative Writing studies and not simply something to teach technique, but to explore the identities we create to write at all.

Michelle Cross in an essay on the popular pedagogies linked with Creative Writing cites R.V. Cassill, founder and first president of the Associated Writing Programs, who is reported by George Garret to have made 'a strong case for the de-institutionalization of creative writing, characterizing the programs as a "a good idea whose time had come and gone"'.[4] Cross suggests that a de-centering of workshop hegemony would remind the writer that the MFA program is 'a fundamentally temporary and contingent community'.[5] August Kleinzahler goes further and has written of the 'creative writing corporation of America.'[6] He's called it 'a billion dollar pyramid scheme'.[7] Others too have voiced reservations about the workshop and the culture it engenders. Most of them have, by the way, taught or worked in a Creative Writing programme of one sort or another.

Of course, there is nothing wrong with a healthy scepticism about Creative Writing workshops, a challenging of its precepts and practices. But, why, others ask, should creativity be an activity which happens in isolation? Artists, fine and graphic, as well as musicians and composers, all work in collaborative spaces, sometimes called master classes, sometimes called workshops. Nobody questions whether students of music benefit from the study of making music, and yet the workshop is all the more a productive space for being contested. It is enriched by the debates surrounding it. Many writers, facilitators and student-writers will find their own desire paths, to use a phrase attributed to Gaston Bachelard. Apprentice writers may be directed a certain way by teachers and workshop-leaders and then it is up them to find their own path. It may not be the one laid down by the academy at all; it may be the other

---

4 Michelle Cross, 'Writing in public: popular pedagogies of creative writing' in Kelly Ritter and Stephanie Vanderslice (eds), *Can it really be taught?: resisting lore in creative writing pedagogy* (Portsmouth, NH, 2007), pp 67–76. Quoted in ibid., p. 11.   5 Ibid., p. 14.   6 August Kleinzahler, Interview with William Corbett, 'The art of poetry No. 93', *Paris Review*, 182 (2007). See: http://www.theparisreview.org/interviews/5789/the-art-of-poetry-no-93-august-kleinzahler, accessed 15 July 2013.   7 Ibid.

less trodden path, not a short-cut, but a deviating, playful path, a line or trajectory suggested by many other forces, cultural or even environmental. In other words, the workshop is not a permanent or immutable rite of passage in a writer's life and I would, therefore, propose one stage in the evolution of the Creative Writing workshop: a word association experiment in what I will call the 'Creative Writing lab' where an apprentice writer can ask questions not just about the craft but about the self, constructed or otherwise, which creates the work.

Unlike the workshop, the Creative Writing lab is a place where the instructor does not supply constructive criticism on a student's work and then invites comments from the students, but creates what Heidi Lynn Staples calls a 'community of practice',[8] where writing is learned rather than taught. Students learn *how to*, rather than *from*. Cultural relativity and a resistance to de-contextualizing an artwork are paramount to Staple's vision of the workshop as a community of practice. The emphasis shifts from the work produced for public consumption to the process of personal transformation. The emphasis is not on craft or technique, but the task of the imagination. The kind of attention one's writing receives in a Creative Writing lab that carries out an experiment like the word association one can challenge the sense of the author's identity and encourage her or him to explore the 'extended' self or the 'self-in-process', to use the expression proposed by Celia Hunt and Fiona Sampson, in order fully to develop their Creative Writing selves.[9]

Here are the procedures for the word association writing experiment (please find the words and grid at the end of this essay):

1. Complete the word association test with a peer.
2. Give as quickly as possible the first word that occurs to you.
3. Your peer marks the words to which you gave a 'delayed' response.
4. Take the 'delayed' words and write a 40-word poem or a 500-word prose piece.

Peer, here, can mean classmate. But the experiment can also be done alone; one student of mine completed the test a second time by herself.

8 Quoted in Paul Perry, *Beyond the workshop* (London, 2013), p. 114.   9 Celia Hunt and Fiona Sampson, *Writing: self and reflexivity* (Basingstoke, Hampshire, 2006), p. 111.

There are many variations to this test which you can devise to suit your own needs, for example deploying fewer or different words. Jung used this test to identify abnormal patterns of response in order to reveal psychological complexes, along with what he called 'intellectual and emotional deficiencies'.[10] As Creative Writing facilitators, we are not looking to identify emotional deficiencies, but to trigger words which will lend the student writer a starting point to delve further into what the constellation of associations might mean to them and amassing words that could lead to the generation of a story or poem. Because the student has been put under time pressure to respond as quickly as she or he can, we can say that the delayed words have a route into the unconscious that a considered response may not elicit.

You could, depending on time, also carry out a 'reproduction test'. In Jung's own words:

> If, after the completion of about one hundred associations, the subject is asked to repeat the original answers to the individual stimulus-words, memory will fail in several places, in such a way that the previous reaction is either not reproduced at all, is given incorrectly, is distorted, or only given after much delay. The analysis of the incorrectly reproduced associations shows that the majority of them were constellated by a complex.[11]

The Creative Writing tutor is not there to supply analysis but merely to facilitate the experiment. It is up to the student writer to devise a creative piece out of the words. A discussion between the student and Creative Writing tutor on why the delayed words bear any significance for the writer can make for interesting discussion and further serve a better understanding of the writing process.

A final stage of the experiment is to write a 1,000 word self-reflective essay on the words you have chosen.

It is worth noting that both Jung and Freud wrote about poets and creative writers. I ask students to read those texts by Jung and Freud and contemporary psychoanalysts like Adam Phillips who has argued that psychoanalysts value poetry more than poets value psychoanalysis,

---

10 C. Jung, 'The Association Method', *American Journal of Psychology*, 31 (1910), 219–69. See http://psychclassics.yorku.ca/Jung/Association/lecture1.htm, accessed 15 July 2013.
11 Ibid.

that poetry is a 'secular bible for psychoanalysts' and that poets, if we accept Freud's assumptions, enjoy their 'daydreams' without the 'self-reproach and shame' of the lay-person.[12] Phillips contends further that psychoanalysts try to turn their patients into 'poets' of their own lives by making known their fantasies and rendering them both acceptable and pleasurable. Freud credited poets with discovering the unconscious before he identified it, after all.

I also point students to various forums and discussion groups which consider the interface of writing and psychoanalysis. For example, recently, the San Francisco Center for Psychoanalysis interviewed a number of poets about what they believed to be the relationship between poetry and psychoanalysis. The poet Brenda Hillmann in her exchange declared that 'most everything we are is the unconscious' and that 'both writers and psychoanalysts strive to be better listeners to what emerges from the unconscious, especially to significant metaphors'.[13] A heightened appreciation of the experience of language is another factor important to both poets and psychoanalysts. For poet Elizabeth Robinson, language is emphasized as an attention to mental states that reflect the intersection between 'the immanent and the transcendent'.[14]

The point of referring students to the secondary reading around the exercise is to encourage them to engage at a deeper level with their own writing and to reflect on the hidden or submerged narrative selves within the matrix created by the trigger words which may yield creative work. There is a certain amount of relinquishment necessary on the student's part: a relinquishment of the conscious tools of composition and a trust in the pool of unconscious prompts our minds can give us. Consideration of the delayed words can also lead to what Antonio Damasio calls an 'extended consciousness' which facilitates greater creativity.[15]

Amber Koski, one of my students, wrote as follows about the experiment:

> Constructing a story using Carl Jung's word association experiment, I was concerned with the narrative feeling unnatural. To

[12] Adam Phillips, *Promises, promises: essays on literature and psychoanalysis* (London, 2002), p. 234. [13] See http://www.sf-cp.org/division-reports/may-2013/poetry-and-psychoanalysis-sfcp-and-j-david-frankel-memorial-fund, accessed 15 July 2013. [14] Ibid. [15] Ibid.

fully understand the experiment, I retook the word association test and found I hesitated over seven of the same words. Too many ideas came to mind when I was given a trigger word, which is something Jung expands on in Lecture I of 'The Association Method'. I often responded with the opposite of the word given. Jung's analysis of this is that the test person has the desire to add something explanatory or supplementary.

I responded to specific words as though they were personal queries about my character, such as: women – trouble, family – broken, money – debt. My responses are ones which for Jung 'conceal or overcompensate for an emotional deficiency'. The repetition of hesitation words during both experiments is an instance when those 'stimulus words strike against special emotionally accentuated complexes'.

The collection of words, as a whole, shows ... how I have retained memories in stimulus words associated with my childhood. Those memories sparked the subject and scene for my story. The collection of stimulus words propelled my mind to one recurring subject: my father ... In using each 'stimulus' word, I was able to construct a narrative connecting the words to a theme or moment relevant to my father. I do not feel that Jung's association test fully addresses the stimulus words and their possible meanings.[16]

The final caveat by this student suggests that it is worth emphasizing that the experiment be seen not as a psychological test, but as a creative writing exercise. It also suggests that discussing what the stimulus or delayed words actually trigger may be helpful. If the experiment aided this student to generate a story which has an emotional meaning for her – it seems to me to be a successful one. Frank O'Connor once wrote that Hemingway's stories illustrated 'a technique in search of a subject'.[17] The purpose of the word association experiment is also to help writers locate a meaningful subject for the technique they will acquire alongside this experiment, whether it is within the same module or another craft-focused one.

16 Amber Koski, MA candidate in Creative Writing and Pedagogy, Kingston University, London, 2012–13.   17 Frank O'Connor, *The lonely voice: a study of the short story* (New York, 2008), p. 36.

As a creative writing tutor, I would not describe as deficiencies or complexes the words the student has delayed on, but simply identify them, discuss their connotative meanings, linguistically and psychologically, consider their imaginative constellations and ask the writer to consider how they may be clues to a narrative he or she could make.

Freud believed that the mind is a poetry-making organ.[18] If we accept this and trust the mind to do its work, it will map out and make connections the conscious self either will not achieve or can set up only pedantically and unimaginatively. The imaginative constellations that the unconscious mind can give us are especially fruitful for writers. Of course, there are many ways of generating material for students to write. However, this method which places the onus on students to reflect on the words around which they have, albeit involuntarily, chosen to construct a poem or story means that there is an added sense of responsibility on their part and an opportunity to reflect on the various impulses and influences which make up their own personal vocabularies and the selves, both authorial and personal, which are constructed by or out of them.

I have resisted calling the word association experiment a game, but I might have done so. The importance of play or the pure *jouissance* of the Creative Writing endeavour is important. Every time I have facilitated the experiment it has been a lot of fun; of course it may bring up rather serious material, but the test subject scenario is one which students relish where they feel emboldened and empowered by what the words they have delayed over might reveal to them.

The writing programme has not seen its end. But there are new ways of re-imagining the workshop as a laboratory where different creative experiments are attempted in an effort to cultivate writers who are more holistically rounded and not bound simply by the mastery of a number of techniques. In this way, writers may emerge who have a greater creative sense of the possibilities of authorship, on and off the page.

---

18 Phillips, *Promises, promises*, p. 222.

APPENDIX: CREATIVE WRITING WORD ASSOCIATION EXPERIMENT SAMPLE SHEET

Word	Response	Reaction Time
head		
frog		
green		
to part		
water		
hunger		
to sing		
white		
dead		
child		
ship		
pencil		
long		
to take care of		
to cook		
union		
clock		
tree		
wind		
whistle		
mow		
laugh		
red		
angel		
cliff		
burgle		
feign		
lake		

'The helmet that never was': reflections on fiction and life writing

CARLO GÉBLER

I

A memory: home (a mock Tudor semi) was 257, Cannon Hill Lane, Morden, London, SW20. My mother was gone. I was living with my younger brother and my father and possibly the Irish au pair.

Items forbidden by my father (this list is not exhaustive): war toys of any kind, especially plastic guns: war comics (these were small, square publications with poor quality black on white illustrations; at school, in the playground, I would occasionally be loaned one of these wonderful publications and afterwards I invariably had smudges on my fingers that smelt intriguingly of industrial ink): Airfix kits (every one a glory): miniature plastic soldiers – about an inch high, these were of every conceivable type from Greek warrior (Trojan War) to Royalist cavalryman (English Civil War) to Prussian grenadier (battle of Waterloo) to artillery officer (American Civil War) to Chindit (Burma campaign, 1941–5).

At school (Hillcross Primary), one summer term (I think my fifth, so I was nine or ten) we did a project on the Second World War and children were instructed to bring in martial objects of World War Two provenance. As a result of this I saw and handled such things as: an officer's belt with a holster, both surprisingly rigid (alas, the holster contained no Webley revolver): a gas mask (this was an incredible object; when I put it on my mouth was filled with the taste of rubber and through the portholes – slightly steamed up – my vision was terrifyingly reduced to just what was immediately in front of me): a gas mask bag (heavy waxed cloth; industrial poppers to hold the flap that closed the top in place; inside, an intriguing system of pouches and sections): a cartridge tin (I assumed it smelt of gun powder but the teacher said no, it was cordite): a full battle dress (British Army; small, surprisingly small; a shade of khaki exactly like wet cardboard; made of some mysterious itchy material that was dense, stiff and, I presumed, unbearably uncomfortable to wear): a dagger in a sheath (ex-Commando and said to have seen active service in Norway; many of us suspected it was actually from Millett's – the camping shop – on Wimbledon Broadway): a private soldier's helmet (British Army, metal; incredibly heavy, wide brim, spherical crown and, inside the crown (revealed when I turned this sacred object over in my hands) an intricate mesh of stained webbing (with adjustable chin strap) which smelt even after so many years – oh how evocative – of the hair oil and sweat of the unfortunate squaddie who had once had this jammed on his head).

After handling these things I was filled with desire. I wanted something real from the war; anything would do just as long as it was authentic. Inevitably my yearning was noticed and one day in the school playground perhaps, or as I walked home along Monkleigh Road, a boy (name forgotten like so many other details in this story) offered me a helmet (US or German, the bulbous type with the bevelled flap around the sides and back at any rate) that his father or someone had carried home in 1945; it wasn't wanted any more he explained, and it could be mine for a small fee. I was desperate. I knew this was a scam but I ignored the inner warnings. How much? He named his figure. It was quite a sum but not so great a sum that I couldn't scrounge, cadge and perhaps even steal it. And I did. I got the money. I don't remember how. But I know that I did. I am sure about that. Then I took the money to school, and my vendor took the money and he explained he would give it to the helmet's owner and then bring the helmet to me. We arranged to meet at an agreed location. My father didn't allow us to wander about at will. However, we went unsupervised to the Children's Library in Morden, so perhaps that was where we agreed to rendezvous. Or perhaps he offered to bring the helmet to school. I forget. And how was I going to smuggle the helmet into 257, Cannon Hill Lane? And where was I going to hide it once I got it in there? I forget that as well. Or maybe I am so ashamed I have suppressed those details. Whatever the case, what I know is we did not meet on the steps of Morden Children's Library, or behind the air raid shelters at the bottom of the Hillcross Primary playing fields where we children traditionally did our financial transactions. My contact never showed up and when I tackled him he denied he had never taken money for a helmet. I was making it up, he said, and I was too timid to challenge him.

Now we get to the important part of the story because this has to do with the writing that came later. My father discovered. He found me out. I don't know how but I do know he had a special talent for uncovering a wayward son's duplicity. Did I have a secret place where I kept my money and did he check it regularly and, finding it empty one day, did he divine the sorry truth? Or did I let the story slip inadvertently? I was a boy who did prattle endlessly. Or did he see me mooning about the house, crying silently, looking depressed? I think this the most likely though I don't actually know: all I know is the end.

I was summoned to his study. It was a warm, male space; there was a big ugly German desk; a stove full of anthracite that whispered as it burnt; a bookcase full of Gorki and Marx and James Stephens; a tallboy; a strong box where he kept our milk teeth and birth certificates; and a bay window with a view over mournful muddy Cannon Hill Common. My father sat, I stood. He'd heard he said, that I'd handed all my money to some imbecile for a helmet and got nothing. 'A bloody army helmet! What were you thinking?' he said.

He followed with questions, lots and lots of them, one after the other: he wanted to know everything, in detail. And I remember, as I stood there, first answering badly, then understanding (but in a dim childish way, and not clearly as I am expressing it here) that what was being sought was the truth, the unvarnished, unreconstructed truth, and then, having had this realization, responding again only this time giving more complex, considered, and accurate replies.

And what I understood, when I reflected on this experience later, and on the numerous other similar occasions when he threw question after question at me in order to ascertain a complete picture of some awful error of mine, was this:

When it came to the exposition of things that had happened to me there were all sorts of different accounts of that event (whatever it was) that I could give; I could give a sad or a funny account, I could give an account that made me look foolish or wise. But if I went further, I realized, if I dug down deeply, dug right down under all these variations, what I came to at the bottom was a sort of bedrock truth, a version of what happened that even a wily, angry sceptic like my father had to concede was what happened because, well, it was the truth as far as it was possible to enunciate the truth, whatever the truth was.

Now I want to be clear; this wasn't an epiphany or series of epiphanies I'm describing: this wasn't something I understood whole and complete at some point in childhood: no, it was something I vaguely ascertained during the scores of interrogations during the unhappy years I lived with my father, and the agglomeration of all these experiences was that I gradually acquired not just the knowledge that it was possible to give a convincing account of what happened, but also the ability to judge the difference between what rung true and what rung false (at least as far as convincing my father went).

In addition, I also learnt a smaller thing in the course of childhood: as part of getting at an experience I learnt how to take people off and replicate (or parody) their talk (a vital skill for later).

2

After a protracted legal struggle my mother secured joint custody of my brother and me: after that we lived part of the week with my father in Morden and the rest with her in Putney. My mother's house was 9, Deodar Road, and one of her neighbours was the English writer Nell Dunn, famous for *Up the junction* (1963), a semi-fictionalized account of working-class life in Battersea. My mother and Nell became friends, while my brother and I became friends with one of her sons (in age he was between my brother and myself): as a result our two families started to spend a great deal of time together.

Deodar Road was a u-shaped loop off the Putney Bridge Road and at the top of the leg on which my mother's house stood (and where Deodar Road hit the Putney Bridge Road) there was a parade of shops where our mothers went to shop rather than Putney High Street. Sometimes Nell would call for my mother and they'd stroll up together (dragging the children along), which was how one afternoon, probably in 1967 when I was nearing thirteen, I found myself standing with them outside the greengrocer. The mothers were talking (I've no recollection of what) when suddenly one of them (Nell, I think) pointed in the direction of Putney High Street and expressed alarm.

I looked and saw an old man striding along the pavement towards us: this was a man on a mission – of that there was no doubt. He wore a raincoat: the buttons were undone so as he moved his coat rose on either side. I'd never seen him before but I now gathered the following:

this was J.R. Ackerley (1896–1967), a writer who lived on the other side of Putney High Street: he was a drunk: he could well be drunk now: he would certainly want to talk: his talk would be interminable: evasive action must be taken immediately.

We fled into the greengrocer. The women went to the rear and turned their backs to the front window. I didn't. I wanted to see more of this man who'd produced such a reaction. I also had a talent for spying, eavesdropping and gathering information without drawing attention to myself (one of the fruits of never having been able to act openly with my father). So I hovered by the door, feigned interest in some fruit or vegetable and waited. Ackerley shot into view: his face was sharp (or so it seemed to me): he had a thin wiry physique: he didn't look at all well: he carried two shopping bags (heavy duty industrial plastic with reinforced handles, the bag type favoured by working-class women as opposed to the raffia or straw jobs decorated with Italian rustic scenes that we used) and these bags were filled with empty soda siphons. I now intuited (or it was subsequently explained) that J.R. Ackerley was taking these to the off-licence further along Putney Bridge Road and with the deposit that would be returned to him for the siphons he intended to buy booze.

This small moment might have got forgotten (would have I don't doubt) except there was an addendum: Nell often lent me books (Maupassant, Sartre, Chekhov and the other Russians) and because of this incident (though not necessarily immediately, this next bit could easily have happened a year or two later) she showed me Ackerley's *Hindoo holiday* (1932), an account of his experiences as private secretary to an Indian maharajah, and she gave me Ackerley's *My dog Tulip* (1956) to read and I did.[1] I'd never read anything like it.

My parents were both writers – of fiction. Nell was a writer – of fiction. Most of the writers with whom my mother and father mixed were writers – of fiction. The house of literature had many splendid rooms but the most splendid of all was the room of fiction; this was the majority opinion.

But *My dog Tulip* was different. Yes, the book used dialogue (the dialogue was brilliant) and many other devices with which I was familiar from novels; yes, it was full of personal facts about feelings,

---

1 Ackerley's most famous work *My father and myself* was not published until 1968 a year after his death: I didn't read this till later.

just like in novels; and yes, this story was saturated with loneliness, something that typically I associated with the novel; only it wasn't a novel. Everything in *My dog Tulip* had happened. It was true.

And not only that, but a person of whom I was in awe, a writer of fiction, Nell (and others like Frances Wyndham who came to my mother's house later and with whom I remember talking about Ackerley) spoke of Ackerley's non-fiction as having as much importance and value as any novel. This revelation made a far greater impression than my discovery about the same time that Ackerley was queer (which was the word used then). I already knew all about what went on in public toilets and London parks so this didn't shock or surprise, though that is not to say I didn't find it interesting. Of course I did. But it was Ackerley's literary practice and the respect he commanded that made the greater impact. Reading Ackerley I discovered that there was another room in the house of literature, hitherto unknown until this moment, the non-fiction room, and once I'd found it I couldn't keep away: I started to go there regularly to borrow and read whatever I could find.

3

In 1968, aged 14, and after a complicated and extremely varied school life (five different schools up to this point) I went to Bedales, a co-educational and enlightened (meaning progressive) institution outside Petersfield, Hampshire. English was compulsory and the first text I was given to read in my English literature class (as opposed to English language) was *A pattern of islands* (1952) by Arthur Grimble (1888–1956), a beautiful elegiac account of the author's life and times first as a cadet administrative officer in the Gilberts and then as Resident Commissioner of the Gilbert and Ellice Islands colony that particularly focused on his relationship with the Kiribati people (the inhabitants of the Gilberts) whose language, Gilbertese, he spoke and whose myths and traditions fascinated him. What struck me about this book was not only the way (like Ackerley) that novelistic techniques were harnessed to the telling of a true story without this seeming jarring or strange, but also the fact that what it was about – the collision between Grimble's European and the Kiribati's Pacific systems of belief – was never overtly stated. *A pattern of islands* showed me that a non-fiction book didn't need to declare its position: it could just be a story like a story in a novel and the meaning or message (whatever it was) could be left implicit for the reader to take if the reader wanted it.

Later, in the same class, reading Laurie Lee's *Cider with Rosie* (1959), and outside the class reading the Blasket Island writers – I particularly adored Maurice O'Sullivan's *Twenty years a-growing* (1933) – I learnt something even more interesting: some writers (like Laurie Lee or Maurice O'Sullivan), eschewing polemic, wrote with words perfectly suited to their subject and, once their words were in my head, mesmerized me as deeply as any novel I loved: and that (which was also Grimble's) was their primary purpose – to move the reader, to make the reader feel. Of course they had a message: both texts were threnodies for an ancient way of life which Lee and O'Sullivan were lucky enough to experience just before its extinction: and both Lee and O'Sullivan regretted (to put it mildly) what was lost: but they didn't offer an argument against progress: they just offered a simple bedrock truth: here is what was lost they said: and experiencing the force of that truth was something I knew I would never forget.

I must add a rider to the above: this understanding that I am ascribing to myself back then was not nearly as clear as I've made it sound. If you'd asked me back then about what we now call life writing my reply would have been muddled and diffuse. Yes, I was groping along the lines I've described, but it's taken me the intervening thirty or so years to get everything straight in my head.

4

I started to earn an erratic living from writing in the mid-nineteen-eighties. My ambition (much as I loved life writing) was to survive by writing fiction. However, on Grub Street, just as in a brothel, it is necessary to offer all services, so I wrote non-fiction; reviews obviously, and, because it was enjoying a renaissance then, quite a bit of travel writing. My travel pieces did involve some life writing (pure narrative shorn of overt ideological intent) but they also (because travel writing is such a mongrel form) involved slabs of history, documentary exposé, journalistic summary, statistics and so on.

The travel articles led in turn to two non-fiction books: *Driving through Cuba* (1988) was a travel book saturated with historical and expositionary material (it could not have been otherwise, the subject after all was revolutionary Castro-governed Cuba): *The glass curtain* (1991) was also a travel book but one where the journey was between political positions rather than places, the subject being Enniskillen and Co. Fermanagh and the effect that political violence had had on the county. There were bits of pure narrative in both these works but these were mixed up with other kinds of writing.

It wasn't until the mid-nineties that I was able to write from life in a pure way. I was working for a film company in Belfast and I used to get the bus up and down to Enniskillen (where I was living, never having left after writing *The glass curtain*). One sultry afternoon in the Enniskillen bus depot an old woman bearded me like the Ancient Mariner beards the wedding guest and spoke at me for half an hour about her loss of faith because of clerical abuse. I was so chastened and galvanized by the encounter I decided I'd write it up. I went to my desk. I could remember what was said. I had a clear memory. It was inside me. My task, I felt, as I began to write, was to make a tracing of something that lived only in memory; this meant I must get the lines on the tracing paper as close to the shape of what was underneath as I could. When I finished the first draft I compared the two: did the lines match the original as I remembered it? When I asked the question I felt I was performing for myself the function my father performed during my childhood interrogations when he forced me to produce a version of the truth that was credible. In other words, my inner critic had something of my father in him: my psyche had taken those childhood interrogations, and appropriated an energy and an attitude from them that it could now use for its own purposes.

When I finished my account of my encounter in the bus depot with the old woman, I took it to the editor of *Fortnight* whose office happened to be above the film company for whom I worked: the editor agreed to take it and asked for another similar piece for the next issue.

Over the next six years, I wrote an 800-word piece based on something I had personally experienced every month (*Fortnight* was a monthly publication despite the name). None of these pieces were invented: they all came from life: they were all true: they had all happened and the pieces were always submitted to the same scrutiny when finished: I would compare the inner memory and the tracing I had made and I would ask did the lines correspond and, if I found they didn't, I'd rub out the lines and re-trace and re-trace until I felt that I'd got the lines as close to the original as I could get them.

5

I always knew I was going to write about my childhood, my relationship with my father, and the consequences and ramifications of that failed relationship for the life I went on to lead as an adult. I knew I would because my father was in me. His beady-eyed capacity to force accuracy was in me. And so was his voice: I could take him off. I also had what I hoped was a good story about us. The only thing stopping me was the feeling that I couldn't and wouldn't do this while he was alive. But then my father died and finally at last I felt free to write.

However, before I started *Father & I* (2000) I made two decisions: first, except in the Prologue, there would be no prescience or foreshadowing: when I wrote about myself at six, say, I would only allow myself to know what I knew when I was six. This decision meant the narrative would have to be chronological but this went with my grain: I've have always favoured stories told in a timely manner as against stories where the writer jerks me around in time. The second decision I made was that I would only include what I remembered: even if I was told by somebody that something had happened, if I didn't remember it, I wouldn't include it.

All that remained now was to do it: I sat down and started and that was when I saw just how valuable writing all those short life pieces for *Fortnight* had been (and I was continuing to produce these even as I wrote and worked on *Father & I*): they had trained me to be really scrupulous with my tracings and I strove very hard when writing *Father & I* to put the lessons learnt into practice and to make what I wrote the most truthful and precise account of what I remembered experiencing that it was in my power to produce.

Of course I also knew it was never going to be authoritative or definitive: it was never going to be *the* truth: it was only going to be the truth as far as it was in my power to recall it: but as long as every word was written in this spirit then I could, I felt, in good faith, offer what I wrote to the reader as the most accurate version of past experience that I was capable of making. And this, it seems to me, having published *Father & I* and done more of this kind of writing subsequently – my last book *Confessions of a catastrophist* (2014) was also a memoir – is what the writer who writes from life must aspire to do always. The work won't ever be perfect and true, or perfectly true, but the effort should always be to get as close to these ideals as it's possible to get.

6

Now I'm in advancing middle age I'm very surprised to find that I've done any life writing at all. I hadn't imagined when I started that I would. I am also gratified; for while it is a pleasure to make something up, it is equally a pleasure to take a lump of unreconstructed experience and to fashion it into something that is both honest to the original experience and yet has the integrity of a literary artefact. I had thought when I started writing that I'd find telling invented stories the supreme pleasure: but what I have discovered is that constructing narratives from life using the literary devices of fiction is just as satisfying. This has to be one of the better surprises that I've had on Grub Street.

Virtual worlds: teaching creative writing in an online environment

NESSA O'MAHONY

One of the great romances of the twenty-first century has been that between the academy and information technology. Universities worldwide have been exploring the potential of technology to streamline the delivery of courses, while at the same time broadening access to a student-base no longer limited to those found locally. Allen and Seaman estimated that in 2005, some three million US students took at least one online course.[1] For their part, more and more students chose to study online because it suits their lifestyles. In their survey of student attitudes towards online courses, Chen, Gonyea and Kuh presented the following findings:

> When asked why they were taking online courses, nearly all distance learners (96%) cited the convenient schedule of these course offerings. Sizeable majorities also indicated that they preferred to work at their own pace (77%) and learn on their own (70%). A third of the learners (35%) reported taking online courses because they did not live near enough to colleges that offer the desired courses, and a fifth of the learners (21%) said that they were seeking less expensive college alternatives. About one in four distance learners (27%) preferred taking courses in this format because they felt that other online learners were more likely to be the same age. Only 8% thought that the grading for online courses would be easier than that for campus-based courses.[2]

Although these findings relate to American students, one could extrapolate similar motivations among distance learners on this side of the

---

[1] Cited in P. Chen, R. Gonyea and G. Kuh, 'Learning at a distance: engaged or not?', *Innovate* 4:3 (2008). See http://www.innovateonline.info/index.php?view=article&id=438, accessed 2 January 2013. The article is reprinted with the permission of the publisher, the Fishler School of Education and Human Services at Nova Southeastern University.   [2] Ibid.

Atlantic. To respond to that perceived need, most Irish and UK universities incorporate some element of online tuition into their courses; the use of technology to provide suitable platforms is here to stay.

How have digital technologies impacted specifically on the teaching of creative writing at third level? I have taught creative writing on a distance learning basis for the Open University in Ireland (OU) for the past five years; in this essay I shall describe one particular undergraduate online Creative Writing course, and will explore the challenges faced and opportunities offered in an online environment when working with students to develop their own writing voices. In a recent newspaper article on the growth of online courses, Ray Schroeder, director of the Center for Online Learning, Research and Service at the University of Illinois, stated that the three things that matter most in online learning are the quality of material covered, the engagement of the teacher and interaction among students.[3] These factors are particularly applicable in the discipline of Creative Writing and there are some interesting things to be learned about community-building and the teacher-student dynamic from the OU course I teach.

A363 Advanced Creative Writing is one of two undergraduate creative writing modules offered by the OU as part of its arts and humanities syllabus. A363 is a Level Three, sixty-point course, and follows on from the Level Two, thirty-point course, A215 Creative Writing. Students taking A363 are assumed to have already taken A215, which offers them an introduction to all aspects of Creative Writing (form, voice, genre, character and setting as applied to poetry, fiction and life writing). A363 has a specific focus on the use of dramatic writing techniques in Creative Writing, and students are guided through the process of writing stage, film and radio scripts, as well as dramatic adaptation. Both A215 and A363 use Virtual Learning Environments (VLEs) to provide the main interface between teacher and students; in each case, there are a number of face-to-face encounters in tutorial format, but the vast majority of interactions take place online.

The OU currently uses a combination of course websites and Moodle (a course management system) as its main VLE for its Creative

---

[3] Laura Pappano, 'The Year of the MOOC', *New York Times*, 2 November 2012. See http://www.nytimes.com/2012/11/04/education/edlife/massive-open-online-courses-are-multiplying-at-a-rapid-pace.html?pagewanted=all&_r=0, accessed 30 December 2012.

Writing courses. Course materials are contained in a published format, with hard-copy posted out to students in their first mailing and a PDF version available for download on the course website. Course materials are also available in alternative formats, including audio and braille. Moodle allows for the creation of discussion threads, known as tutor group forums; these forums are moderated by each tutor and students use them to post exercises contained in the course book, or set for them by their tutor. They can also use these forums to post work they are developing for continuous assessment; A363 students are expected to complete six Tutor Marked Assignments (TMAs) over the course of the academic year, and an End of Module Assignment (EMA) to complete their assessed work.

With so much course activity taking place on the discussion forums, this style of teaching and learning will suit some students more than others. Participating in an OU course requires a certain level of computer proficiency, and the Creative Writing courses, with their discussion forums and threads where students can post work in progress and receive feedback from fellow students, are more digitally-intensive than most. And yet it is possible to take A363 without any access to IT whatsoever; the OU has a number of prisoners among its student cohort, the majority of whom cannot access the internet and so must follow the course materials in printed form. Although this can place them at a disadvantage, in my experience they often overcome such limitations with impressive results. I believe the major reason that off-line students can perform so well is due to the quality of the written course material, something that Ray Schroeder cited as integral to the success of any online course.[4] The *Advanced creative writing* course book (edited by Derek Neale with contributions from Bill Greenwell and Linda Anderson) is an impressive and detailed manual, with excellent exercises and a thoughtful and provocative accompanying anthology of excerpts from creative texts.[5] The companion website leads the students through the chapters and activities week by week, and there is a printed study guide that provides the same direction to off-line students. However, while it is possible to take this course without computer access, the online element adds a whole new dimension for participating students.

4 Ibid. 5 Derek Neale (ed.), *A creative writing handbook: developing dramatic technique, individual style and voice* (London, 2009).

Online teaching relies on the engagement of both teachers and students, and I believe that the success of any presentation of the A363 course rides on the ability of the teacher to develop a sense of community among the students as the academic year progresses. Because we meet in the flesh so rarely (there are two face-to-face tutorials, the first at the beginning of the course and the second half-way through the year), it is vitally important that students build a sense of trust, both between themselves and their teacher, but also with each other. Experienced OU teachers have developed a whole range of tools to help foster that sense of community; these ice-breakers include using acrostics as introductions to each other, quizzes around the first lines of famous novels and even posting extracts of one's own work in progress for feedback from students. I have been lucky to have many generous colleagues who have been prepared to share such techniques with me. In fact, that sense of collegiality and mutual support is fostered by the online environment; as teachers, we have our own discussion forum on Moodle, where we can compare notes, query problems and generally share teaching approaches. I have found that an invaluable source of support over the past few years.

How does one develop a sense of community among a group of comparative strangers, who don't have an option to go for coffee or the bar after a lecture, and who are expected to hit the ground running in terms of online participation? A363 work is allocated over a thirty-week period from early October to late May, and students are set weekly tasks alongside the preparatory work for each assignment. The quicker a group gets to trust each other, the sooner they are in a position to offer fair and detailed critiques of each other's postings. I should explain that there is a considerable degree of peer-critiquing in this course. The majority of the OU's tutors are part-time staff, and each course has a set number of student contact hours and a weekly average of work hours. Because of the limited time available, the main focus of my activity as tutor is reserved for marking assignments, answering queries and running the face-to-face and online tutorials. Other work posted by students (course book activities or drafts for assignments) will only be commented upon by fellow students, unless a student requires me to answer a specific query in relation to a piece of work posted. In an environment where peer-feedback is essential, students will be more likely to critique each other if they have some sense of where their fellow students are coming from.

Tutors in distance learning courses need to be very proactive in the early stages of any course presentation in order to begin to build that sense of community. OU tutors write to each of their students at the very beginning of the course, to introduce themselves and to give students some idea of how they are likely to run the module over the course of the year. When I first joined the OU, tutors were expected to write letters to students to their home addresses; gradually this has evolved to the point where I can now send group-emails to students, welcoming them onto the course and giving them information about when I am likely to be logging on, what my contact hours are and the sort of participation they can expect from me over the year.

This opening letter is also a useful tool for setting boundaries; for example, it is a common assumption among distance learning students that their tutors are always online and thus always ready for an instantaneous response to any query. In my welcome note I explain that I will only be logging on at certain times of the week, and will endeavour to answer queries as promptly as I can; this it is hoped deflects any unrealistic expectations about availability on the part of my students. I also make reference to issues of 'netiquette'; the sorts of behaviours I do and don't expect on online discussion forums. While many students are familiar with protocols such as not writing entire postings in capital letters (which means shouting) and keeping their tones as moderate and dispassionate as possible, it is always important to remind them of the power of the written word and that nuances don't always translate; off the cuff responses rarely work on discussion forums. This was something that Heather Beck felt necessary to point out to her students when developing her online MA course in novel writing for Manchester Metropolitan University:

> I also remind them that messages posted to the bulletin board are more formal than face-to-face or online live seminar chat exchanges, so it's wise to take special care regarding tone when giving feedback.[6]

---

6 Heather Beck, 'Teaching creative writing online', *New Writing: the international journal for the practice and theory of creative writing*, 1:1 (2004), 26. See http://dx.doi.org/10.1080/14790720408668189, accessed 27 December 2012.

Thus far I have been lucky enough to avoid any significant flame-throwing incidents between students on my discussion forums. The most serious problem I encountered was the habit of one student, when giving feedback, of simply re-writing and editing other students' drafts and posting her versions on the forum. It can be tempting to rewrite other's work in the way we ourselves would write it, and the presence of an electronic draft posted on an online forum makes that temptation harder to resist. Although this student was an excellent editor, it took several email exchanges, and some very annoyed comments from the other students, before I could convince her that it was not the most helpful way of offering a critique, and that she would be better off pointing out perceived problems in general terms so that the others could find their own solutions to the issue. The ability to both predict and stave off any problems before they occur, and dampen down fires that do erupt, is an important skill for the online tutor.

In the welcome letter, I also provide details of our first face-to-face tutorial, which generally is scheduled to happen within a couple of weeks of the course opening. It is important, I think, for the first face-to-face tutorial to happen quite swiftly, while students are still finding their feet. It is also important that these first tutorials are planned carefully, to allow students to refresh their memories about some of the main ideas covered over the previous course, while beginning to grapple with the very specific challenges of dramatic writing techniques that feature in A363. Students also have a genuine curiosity about their teacher, so a face-to-face meeting helps them understand where I am coming from as a tutor and it allows me to get an initial sense of their interests, proclivities and focuses as writers. Thus face-to-face tutorials will comprise ice-breaking exercises, general discussion, reading and exercises responding to specific aspects of the course. Students are invited to post any work that emerges from the tutorial on the online discussion forums. This ensures that the momentum, not to mention the sense of camaraderie, established at the face to face tutorial is continued into the online environment.

In my experience, tutors on online courses that lack any element of face-to-face participation find it much harder to build a sense of community. Another course I previously taught for the OU was a short, ten-week one entitled Start Writing Fiction (A174), which has since ceased presentation. There were no face-to-face tutorials in this course, and students never got a chance to meet each other. Although there was some forum participation, students were far less likely to post their own work or comment on that of others, even though the course was designed to encourage students to post exercises and give feedback to each other. Admittedly, the short nature of the course also worked against the development of any sense of real community, but I remain convinced that students were also reticent because they had no sense of who their fellow students were and were thus reluctant to share their work online.

A363 students can sometimes exhibit similar reticence, usually when the course is well under way and they are unable to sustain the enthusiasm for posting exhibited during those first weeks. At that point, the tutor needs to find imaginative ways of attracting them back to the discussion forums, while recognizing that there are some points when students simply need to be allowed to develop their creative ideas in the solitary space we writers all need to inhabit. The forums themselves should be designed to offer students as much flexibility as possible for online discussion. There are dedicated threads set up for discussion of general issues arising from the course materials; there are also distinct threads where they can post activities in response to the various sections in the course handbook and a separate thread for assignment work in progress but there should also be a space for more relaxed chatting. I create a thread called 'the Green Room' where students can dip in and out and talk about whatever they like. This has the advantage of preventing other discussion threads degenerating into general chatter because students know they have somewhere to go for the more social end of things; I make it clear that I won't be moderating that particular thread and leave the students to it. But for the most part, students are made aware that the course places specific emphasis on their developing both self-reflective and critiquing skills; the discussion forums give them the opportunity to gather the necessary material.

The coursework is also designed to promote self-reflection and critiquing. Five of the six assignments, as well as the end of module project, involve the production of a piece of creative work, along with a commentary reflecting on the process of writing it. The sixth assignment, which occurs third in the cycle of assessment tasks, requires students to write a critical reflection of work and commentaries that have been posted by their fellow students on the tutor group forum. Prison-based students, and others who cannot access the discussion forums, are provided with a 'mock-forum' in PDF format which contains discussion threads manufactured by the course team. The idea here is to stimulate the students' critical faculties, and to encourage them to engage with texts other than their own while demonstrating that they have absorbed the lessons of the course and can analyse how well their colleagues' pieces are working.

Not surprisingly, there is occasional student dissatisfaction with this particular task; some simply cannot see the point of having to offer a critique of a fellow student's work, while others find it embarrassing or feel curtailed, even though they are aware that their colleagues will not be reading their appraisals because students are not encouraged to post draft TMA03s online. But most students eventually come to realize the value of this particular assignment; they understand that learning to evaluate another writer's work and then write critically about it helps them refine their own process as writers and self-reflective critics. Students who have fully engaged with this particular task tend to write much stronger commentaries in subsequent assignments. But the varying reactions to the task hint at a larger issue that often surrounds the existence of online discussion forums; that issue is related to group dynamics.

The influence of group dynamics can come into play in any type of workshop situation, real or virtual. I have facilitated many real life workshops over the years, and know the extent to which personalities can influence the direction, not to mention the success or failure, of a workshop. Sometimes one or two over-dominant types can take over the classroom, and it takes careful handling to ensure that other quieter souls are not intimidated or excluded. At least when the tutor is in the room with the students, she can read body language and pick up on nuances to judge whether any redirection is needed. But this is much more difficult in an online environment, where you cannot see the reactions of other students to particularly dominant posters. 'Radio silence', or the complete absence of postings, on a discussion forum could be caused by a wide range of factors: life gets busier suddenly; there's a family crisis; the student has fallen behind gradually and is now daunted by the productivity of others in the class; or else is simply intimidated by what they perceive as an aggressive or overly critical approach by one of their colleagues. As a tutor, I can use Moodle-tools such as the one that allows me to know how recently a student has logged on and to see which students have read what posts, but it requires on-going vigilance to ensure that I am not simply overlooking those students who have not posted recently, and who have not got in touch with me to let me know they have a problem. It is good practice to send periodic messages, either via email or on the tutor group forum, inviting people to get in touch with queries or to let me know of any issues that are arising; students may not be proactive, but are often glad to take up the offer of help if the tutor extends one.

The interesting counterpoint to the problem of students who do not participate in the forum is the frustration experienced by more active students who post regularly but feel they are not getting reciprocity. More than one student has complained to me that they could not see the point in offering extensive feedback to other students because they rarely got anything back in return; indeed, they might feel particularly resentful that they were generating plenty of material for other students to use in the TMA reserved for student critiques but were not being given feedback by way of exchange. In these cases, I try to persuade them that mutuality is the basis of all good workshops, and then look for ways in which I can encourage other quieter students to participate in the online discussions. Although it is a constant temptation for a tutor to allow online workshops that have a few active students to tick over, merely intervening when a crisis arises, I have found that more constant monitoring and intervention can help to prevent those crises occurring in the first place.

As I mentioned previously, the A363 course is structured to combine continuous assessment with one, larger project, which is developed over the latter part of the course and then completed as an End of Module Assessment (EMA). Much of this developmental work is carried out during the final two months of independent study built into the course. But here too the course designers have given careful thought to finding ways of providing students with skills that they would need in the real world of writing. Thus while the fourth assignment asks them to make a proposal for the EMA, the fifth assignment asks them to produce a piece of creative work entirely unrelated to the EMA, before returning with a draft extract from the EMA for their sixth and final assignment. When students query why they are simply not allowed to work on the EMA for the remainder of the course, I point out that writers frequently find themselves having to work on parallel projects and that it is a good discipline to be able to compartmentalize; the metaphor of plate-spinning comes in useful in this context! During this period the students can continue to post work in progress and discuss issues as they arise on the tutor group forum, while I, as tutor, continue carefully to monitor, answer queries and intervene when the need arises.

Forum moderation is only one part of an online teacher's role; the other significant part is in the actual assessment of students' work. Assessment in a distance learning environment has its own particular challenges and opportunities. As I explained earlier, given the limited amount of time available to the part-time tutor within the OU framework, feedback on assignments is one of the main teaching tools available to reinforce the core learning outcomes from the A363 course. The OU asks us to use a combination of general summaries and annotated feedback when marking scripts. I have found it invaluable to use a general template for each summary sheet, that has specific sections for strengths, where the assignment could be improved, what grade has been received and, most importantly, what it could have done to score more highly, and finally what I am expecting to see in the next assignment. You might think that this could lead to a lot of repetition in terms of feedback, but I have discovered that having that template allows me to tailor my comments to the individual needs of the student much more succinctly than if I had started from scratch each time. However, it is in the annotated feedback part of the assessment that I feel I am having an actual conversation with each student. I comment as I read, giving the student the benefit of my first impressions and then I revise my comments having re-read the piece in its entirety. This process comes as close as I can to actually having a consultation with the student – it is the distance learning equivalent to the office hours meeting in a bricks and mortar university. I try to be as detailed as I can be in my feedback; it is vital that students find my comments useful in going forward with their next project. It is made clear to them that they can query any comment or aspect of my feedback with me afterwards by email or by posting to the forum; my annotations are part of an on-going dialogue between tutor and students.

But one area that I try to get them less fixated on is the actual grade they receive for a piece of work, although I am probably on a hiding to nothing in this regard. I know from my own experience, having been a creative writing Masters student, about the highs and lows experienced when receiving grades, and yet as a teacher I also know the subjectivity that can lie at the basis of many grading decisions. Of course there are grading bands, assessment guidelines and course criteria to consider, but I have attended enough marking moderation meetings to know that there can be considerable variations among markers; one woman's first might be another's third, with both markers arguing their case passionately. I tell my students that they only receive marks because they are studying as part of an academic course where assessment must receive some kind of recognizable scoring; but they rarely listen (nor did I!). While the grading issue is not unique to the online teaching of Creative Writing, the subject of grades takes up an inordinate amount of student discussion on the green-room forums; for that reason, the OU has placed a ban on specific discussion of grades, although students will always find ways around it. A363 group Facebook pages are not a place for the unwary tutor to wander during assignment-marking time.

I believe that there are both advantages and disadvantages when it comes to teaching Creative Writing in an online environment. Although the lack of a human dimension can be problematic, the use of online discussion forums that build a sense of community and that encourage students to be not only self-reflective but also helpful peer critics can have important and long-lasting benefits. There is a pleasing democracy in such an approach, as Heather Beck notes:

> Marcelle Frieman ... at Macquarie University in Australia argues how the teaching methodology of creative writing promotes student-centred learning with interactions between students being as important as those between students and tutors. In this way, students increasingly see tutors not so much as experts but as facilitators for their own learning. Frieman's online teaching suggests that the student-centred learning characteristic of creative writing transfers well to online environments.[7]

---

7 Heather Beck, 'Teaching creative writing online', 33.

Furthermore, Sarah Guth has pointed to the pedagogical value of peer-feedback, citing scholars who argue that 'peer readers can provide useful feedback that tends to be different from and more specific than teacher feedback.'[8] Some of my most satisfying moments as an OU tutor have been when I have observed students on the discussion forums helping each other with queries, and providing more astute advice that I might have given in similar circumstances. I see my role as combining guidance, moderation and facilitation in the sometimes daunting, but never dull, virtual world of online Creative Writing teaching. As an online tutor, I share the ambition of all Creative Writing teachers: to help my students to become the best writers that they can be.

---

8 Sarah Guth, 'Discovering collaborative e-learning through an online writing course', *Innovate*, 3:2 (2006). See http://ww.innovateonline.info/index.php?=article&Id=277, accessed 3 January 2013.

'The Man in the Moon's autobiography': memoir and the creative writing workshop

EIBHEAR WALSHE

In a letter to his friend Patrick Swift, written in 1960, John McGahern discussed the novel he was then writing and, while doing so, sought anxiously to establish the relationship between episodes in his own life and various key elements in his fiction. In defining these connections, McGahern was characteristically forthright, even vehement, about the vital difference, as he saw it, between memoir and fiction writing:

> But the autobiographical stunt! Very few of the situations in the book ever happened in my life – in that sense, it is no more mine than the Man in the Moon's autobiography. THE WHOLE BOOK owes everything to my experience, the way I suffered and was made to laugh, the people I have lived among, the landscape and the books I liked ... But it is seldom possible to be ourselves in real life ... the common notion that you can make an art out of your life, refinements of pleasure, etc, is pure moonshine as far as I can see. There must be some morality.[1]

McGahern drew extensively on his own life experience in his successive novels and stories, using the landscape of his Leitrim childhood, the traumatic experience of his beloved mother's early death and the burdensome presence of his domineering father as key elements with which to begin his own process of fiction-making. However, right at the beginning of his writing career, he made a clear distinction between the use of personal experience in the composition of a work of fiction and the very different genre of memoir or autobiographical writing. He resisted the idea that creating fiction was a simple process of writing the self into a thinly disguised narrative form. It is worth noting that McGahern waited until he had stopped writing novels and stories to publish his memoir. Fiction often grows from autobiograph-

---

[1] Denis Sampson, *Young John McGahern: becoming a novelist* (Oxford, 2012), p. 131.

ical experience, but, in the process, as McGahern suggests, it needs to undergo a thorough process of refashioning. For writers like McGahern, using a moral perspective was the key method of filtering and transforming the raw material of felt life into a new form, and thus creating a new fictive world. Given this difference, I would argue that memoir writing stands in a very unique position in relation to other forms of Creative Writing. As McGahern indicates, personal experience is often, perhaps always, a crucial part of the imaginative process. Poetry, drama and prose can all involve some degree of writing of the self, but there is always the convention of the imagined world to screen any direct connection between the writer and her/his life. A novel, a play or a poem can mask or disguise the autobiographical source, if necessary. But by its nature, memoir stands unprotected. It is, or so its very title seems to proclaim, the unvarnished, pre-fictionalized truth about the inner and outer life of the writer, an un-cracked looking glass into the soul of the subject.

The convention that life writing is unvarnished truth is on a par with the other convention that fiction is pure invention. Experienced writers come to the genre of memoir writing with a keen sense of self-protection, and they often use sleight of hand to disarm the reader with protestations of fading powers of observation, an unsteady pen and their own flawed powers of remembrance. One of my favourite memoirs, and one I always use in creative writing workshops, is Kate O'Brien's *Presentation parlour,* published in 1962. This was written when her professional career as a novelist had come to an end and it is a beguiling account of her Limerick childhood, told through the figures of her five beloved aunts. O'Brien opens her memoir with a beautifully lyrical disclaimer, presenting her task as self-biographer as if her memoir was already a failure, falling down in the task of recollection, of recording and of honest portrayal:

> My recollections are not pure. Time and myself have worked upon my aunts for me, and the portraits I have sketched are perhaps not portraits even in the freest, most expressionist sense, for anyone but me. And even for me, there are not representational or within sight of being photographic. The time is too long; I peer through half-shut eyes from very far away, and the knowingness of adult life cannot help but throw in accents and

shadows which the child who knew these women could not have perceived.²

In fact, *Presentation parlour* is a skilled, entertaining and successful autobiography because, in the course of the narrative, O'Brien manages to protect and elide her own contentious adult life most efficiently. She celebrates those elements of her Catholic childhood and middle-class upbringing she cherished most. The disclaimer at the beginning, the plea for a kind of absolving, is a clever way of disarming the reader into acceptance of evasions by a writer still at the height of her powers.

I often use this opening paragraph from Kate O'Brien within the Creative Writing workshop to signal to participants that there can be potentially intimidating expectations of honesty, revelation or painful disclosure in life writing. However, I go on to suggest that it can be liberating to realize that this expectation has been played with and evaded by the most successful memoirists. This leads to the discussion that learning how to write a memoir in a workshop should, by the nature of the genre, take a different course from other classes on varying modes of Creative Writing. This is so because the student in a creative writing class on memoir has to come to terms very quickly with the idea that all forms of writing are revelation. I remind them of Oscar Wilde's perception that all portraits painted with feeling are portraits of the artist and not of the sitter and indicate that they will learn to be self-aware about potential embarrassment, hurt or fear in relation to their own writing. However, I always make the point that the teaching of memoir in the classroom has a great deal in common with other forms of creative expression in that it centres on recall, and on the process of capturing in words memories, sensations or visual images that surface during the process of recollection. Many of the exercises we explore in the Creative Writing workshop share in the processes associated with all forms of Creative Writing and, to a degree, participants can begin writing with the realization that memoir is the genre they have provisionally chosen, but they can later decide to recast their autobiographical writing into fiction, the short story form or drama.

In leading classes in life writing in arts centres and community groups, I discuss the process of recall and writing, and always include

---

2 Kate O'Brien, *Presentation parlour* (London, 1963), p. 5.

an account of my own experience of writing and publishing memoir. Wilde declared that 'the highest as the lowest form of criticism is a mode of autobiography'.[3] For me, critical and biographical writing led to the experience of memoir writing and, as a result, the teaching of life writing in workshops. My first attempt at memoir writing came after many years of working in the field of literary criticism and Irish writing and was a direct result of my experience of editing a biography.

In the early 2000s, I was working on a biography of Kate O'Brien, a task fraught with difficulty because of lack of access to archives and also because of contentious debates around her sexuality. When I had finished my first draft, one or two readers pointed out to me that there was very little sense in it of the person or individual, and that I needed to describe, as much as I could, Kate O'Brien both as a public and a private self within my biography. To remedy this, I decided that I would write a short pen picture as an exercise to see whether I was capable of performing this task of character description. I decided that I would try to produce an account of someone distinctive, whose characteristics and mode of speech and self-presentation were well known to me. I sat down and wrote a short description of my late grandmother, Cissie, who had died fifteen years previously. I found that what had begun as a task now became a great pleasure. The writing flowed very easily, I enjoyed revising it and capturing as nearly as I could, her remembered voice, her mannerisms and her way of inhabiting her world. Energized by this experiment, I then went back to the Kate O'Brien biography, revised that book in light of that experience of life writing before it was published.

Writing that fragment of description alerted me to something. It was the realization that I had begun to write a portrait of someone I had never encountered anywhere else in a book, particularly in an Irish memoir. Cissie was unique, to me, and I was confident in my selective and deliberately likeable representation of my witty, glamorous little grandmother, and so I decided to return to this new writing process. I wanted to expand the memoir, to include other elements from my childhood and, in some way, to bring my own childhood and adolescence back. To do this, recollected physical spaces were crucial for my remembering, writing and editing while the memoir grew. I devoted

---

3 Oscar Wilde, *The picture of Dorian Gray* (New York, 2007), p. 3.

an hour every morning to the writing and decided to shape each chapter as much as I could around a building. I found that if I concentrated on memories of specific buildings in 1960s Waterford, on dining rooms, particular streets, shops (mainly cake shops!), churches, hospitals, schools and libraries, then the visual aspect of these places grounded the experience of memory recall for me and allowed the writing to emerge. Closing my eyes and entering a room or walking down a street in Waterford made the past more accessible as I prepared to write early each morning. However, I found that I didn't want to return to those places as they are now, preferring to revisit them solely in my mind's eye.

If this sounds as if I was simply channelling the past, well, that was just one part of the process and an initial part as well. As I explain in class, these primal materials of recollection then needed to be shaped, re-arranged and sometimes changed to fit the structure of the memoir and the demands, as I saw it, of the pace of the story and the portrait of myself that I was preparing to unfold. Often events that had happened to others in my family were now co-opted to become my experience and, in this, I am always honest. The making of a memoir is a process of filtering and of re-arrangement, just as much as the making of fiction, poetry and drama.

As I kept on writing, with no plan in mind, just a sense of enjoyment, I found the memoir began to expand to include the entire city of my childhood. Another aspect of this recalling came as I began to replay conversations from my childhood in my head, rehearsing words, accents and intonations aloud to myself, and watching, inside my head, as I conjured up some of the scenes and moments I remembered. Part of my desire to write about my own past was a common one for the whole genre of memoir, the wish to experience the primary moment of recall and then to attempt to put that memory down on paper, with the future possibility for others to read and, hopefully, to experience it. This is, I think, the key impulse driving most autobiographical writing. For me, another element was my growing sense that I had never read accounts of any other gay childhood in the many Irish memoirs I had studied or taught. It is part of the impulse that also lies behind my other academic work: recovery projects like my study of Oscar Wilde and Ireland, or my book on Kate O'Brien, are driven by the curiosity to rediscover lost or hidden histories. I wrote the memoir because I wanted to read a memoir like this myself. I also didn't want it to be a misery memoir, or full of self-pity or recrimination. It was to be a story of survival and of successful self-realization and this also shaped the way in which I tailored and remade the raw materials of memory.

The memoir was published and reviewed. I read it on RTÉ radio but none of the expected storm happened, at least not the one I was dreading in darker moments when I thought about the move from my computer to book form. As a result of seeing it in print, I decided that I wanted to start teaching workshops in memoir writing, confident that I could share some of my own experience of this kind of writing and that training as a teacher would give me the ability to communicate my methods of composition and thus enable participants to connect with their own particular voices and the forms of expression that best facilitated their own writing.

In teaching memoir writing, I use the structure of the three-hour workshop, usually on a Saturday morning. So far, I have run workshops purely for enjoyment and self-fulfilment, outside the context of the university. Therefore, they are not graded or assessed. This is a vital liberation: the participants are there to write for pleasure, for self-expression and for fulfilment; the atmosphere is relaxed and can be helpful, sympathetic and supportive. To begin, I use extracts from Irish memoirs, including O'Brien's *Presentation parlour*, Wilde's *De profundis*, Elizabeth Bowen's *Seven winters* and Sean Ó Faoláin's *Vive moi*. Discussing the elusive nature of memory is my way into the process of writing the self and the following celebrated passage from Proust is always a starting point and not just because he gave me a sense of permission that grandmothers could be part of literary writing. Although Proust was describing the magical, elusive and transformative power of random memory for fiction, his account of this process is just as relevant to the quest involved in memoir writing. He articulates the miracle of memory as a means by which time can be transcended and conquered:

> And soon, mechanically, dispirited after a dreary day with the prospect of a depressing morrow, I raised to my lips a spoonful of the tea in which I had soaked a morsel of the cake. No sooner had the warm liquid mixed with the crumbs touched my palate than

a shudder ran through me and I stopped intent upon the extraordinary thing that was happening to me. An exquisite pleasure had invaded my senses, something isolated, detached, with no suggestion of its origin. And at once the vicissitudes of life had become indifferent to me, its disasters innocuous, its brevity illusory – this new sensation having had on me the effect which love has of filling me with a precious essence; or rather this essence was not in me it *was* me. I had ceased now to feel mediocre, contingent, and mortal. Whence could it have come to me, this all-powerful joy? I sensed that it was connected with the taste of the tea and the cake, but that it infinitely transcended those savours, could not, indeed, be of the same nature. Whence did it come? What did it mean? How could I seize and apprehend it?[4]

In class, I suggest that this is a key way into the writing of memoir, the intangible, powerful link between sensory perception and hidden memory and so we use a variety of methods to explore memory. Often I start with the idea of a room, a place significant in the past. I ask participants to close their eyes and envisage this room, preferably a place no longer accessible to them in everyday life, perhaps in another city or no longer in existence, yet, at the same time, indelibly part of their past. Using this image of the room, I ask the participants to write a brief description, a page or so, to recall the room, its size, furnishings, and the ways in which light falls into it. Using excerpts of work by Elizabeth Bowen or Virginia Woolf, I look at other examples of rooms in fiction. I always instruct that the remembered room is imagined as empty, silent, unobserved: in other words, existing only in the past and only capable of being re-animated through individual recollection. With this first draft in hand, I ask participants to put down their pens, read it and then pick up the pen and make any emendations that occur. Then I suggest another, fresh blank page and a new draft, re-inscribing the same description, but this time altering and editing it. One of the advantages of having three hours to work on a single exercise is that the participants can make at least three drafts and can also read the last draft aloud. This allows the rest of the group, including myself, to comment and commend but also to suggest ways in which editing can concentrate the

[4] *Remembrance of things past. Volume 1: Swann's way*, trans. C.K. Scott Moncrieff and Terence Kilmartin (New York, 1999), pp 48–51.

description of the room, focus and intensify the images called up. Then, I ask participants to bring home that final draft, type it up and make copies for us all for the next class. In this way, the student can see the shift from a handwritten draft to a finished typed copy and also the rest of the group will see the piece develop and take shape. Using this one remembered physical space, I then set up a series of exercises around it: the creation of descriptions of the songs or music heard there, conversations recalled, food tasted, scents and smells or the colour, fabrics and textures of clothes worn by those inhabiting that room. On the process of writing and re-writing, I am always reminded of a story told by the novelist, Mark Haddon, who said that the best question he was ever asked about his work came at a reading for a group of children. One child asked him if writing was really all about crossing out. It certainly is: I try to build in a process of drafting, redrafting, reading aloud, taking advice and reaction and then typing and retyping into each workshop. At the basis of the creative workshop in life writing is the pursuit of the same raw materials of fiction, drama and poetry, the writing of the physical, the evocation of food, song, and clothes and of ways of inhabiting the physical world.

To finish our series of workshop classes, I often invite reflection on the final sentences of Kate O'Brien's memoir, an elegiac disavowal of her own powers of autobiographical writing. They seem an appropriate way to conclude this discussion of the purpose and ambition of writing the self:

> So there they pass, my aunts. No one but I will care about their 'short and simple annals'. Yet it has rested with me to set them down, and to try and find in their modest lives the essence of them. That I have not done ... And for all my searching back, for all my will to reach them, I have not found the heart of any one of them. So now I can only say goodbye to them, ask them to forgive my impertinent affection, my vulgar probing, and wish that they rest forever in peace.[5]

---

5 Kate O'Brien, *Presentation parlour*, p. 138.

Ars longa, vita brevis: the novel, the workshop and time

ÉILÍS NÍ DHUIBHNE

'I HATE TALKING ABOUT WRITING THE NOVEL'

'Ah, I hate talking about writing the novel.'[1] Thus opens an article on the novel by Graeme Harper, one of the most experienced professors of Creative Writing as an academic subject. He goes on to compare the act of writing a novel to travelling in space, and the process of learning to write a novel to learning to ride the waves on a surfboard (that is, a combination of skill and instinct is required).

Teaching any genre of writing is challenging. In the new university programmes in Creative Writing which have blossomed in Ireland over the past fifteen years, the teacher is almost always a writer who has not taken a Creative Writing degree herself, and is learning to teach on the job. She must fire on many cylinders. She should inspire creativity and nurture talent, create an atmosphere in which students are free to experiment and change, while at the same time providing constructive criticism, editing, grading and imparting knowledge about literature, literary theory and writing theory. These conditions apply to the teaching of every genre of writing. But teaching the novel poses additional challenges and is the most demanding literary form with which to work in the context of the workshop or classroom.

To judge from the multiplicity of novel writing courses that are on offer, this is not a widely-held view. If you are seeking instruction on how to write a novel, plenty of classes are available, in the university, in the community, on islands in the Mediterranean, and online. Indeed, it's easy to get the impression that the vast majority of Creative Writing courses are concerned with this genre in particular. And there is little doubt that the ambition of many, perhaps the majority, of apprentice writers is to write, then publish, a novel, the genre which is seen to represent the pinnacle of fictional achievement, which is the

---

[1] Graeme Harper, 'The novel' in Graeme Harper (ed.), *Teaching creative writing* (London, 2006).

most popular among readers, and which can win the greatest worldly success for its authors.

In the graduate programmes in Creative Writing in University College Dublin, which were established in 2006, the teaching of the writing of the novel follows two pedagogical models, and two kinds of classroom experience. The first is the taught module, which leans in the direction of the traditional academic product- or knowledge-based model. The second is a process-based, studio or workshop model, 'emphasizing activities and effects',[2] the classic method of the earliest Creative Writing programmes, such as that established first in the Iowa Writers' Workshop in 1936[3] and which flourished as the Creative Writing programme developed in American universities from the 1950s on. Both these teaching models have advantages and disadvantages as far as the teaching of the novel is concerned.

The taught module provides a structured approach to teaching the novel; it focuses on theoretical aspects of writing such works, illustrating theory with examples from texts. Students taking this module read a number of novels, discuss key aspects such as voice, point of view, characterization, dialogue, and so on. They will also submit some of their own work for review and discussion – an element of workshop is thus incorporated into the structured class.

In the second model, the novel workshop, participants practise and hone their writing skills under supervision. Students present extracts from their own work for review and discussion – typically chapters. These are read in advance of the workshop by all participants, and reviewed or workshopped. Ideally each student's work will receive at least half an hour's attention each time they present. Theoretical aspects may be discussed informally, as such issues arise in the course of the specific reviews.

When the taught theoretical module is the teaching model, the first challenge for the teacher is that the novel, even more than most literary genres, is hardly a single genre at all, but a spectrum of related sub-genres, like an enormous extended family. By comparison, the short story is not just a lonely voice, but an only child. The novel is like the

2 M. Neary, 'Curriculum models and developments in adult education', *Curriculum studies in post-compulsory and adult education: a teacher's and student teacher's study guide* (Cheltenham, 2003), pp 57–70.   3 Mark McGurl, *The program era: postwar fiction and the rise of creative writing* (Cambridge, MA, 2009), p. 5.

species 'dog': it includes everything from Alsatians to toy poodles – because we have a Platonic idea of 'dog', we are able to classify many breeds which look completely different from one another as belonging to the same species. So it is with novels. Short stories are more like cats. There are many varieties but they all look pretty similar. (For the purposes of this simile, it's necessary to forget about antecedents and cousins in the wild, the wolves and tigers, folk tales and legends.) The contemporary Irish short story is still by and large written in the mode of early modernism – realistic, lyrical, Chekhovian-Joycean models predominate[4] – and almost always belongs to the category of fiction we describe as literary, as opposed to popular or commercial. Although Donald Barthelme already in 1964 dismissed this kind of story as a 'constructed mouse-trap like to supply, at the finish, a tiny insight typically having to do with innocence violated',[5] it is still the most usual form of the short story. Novels, on the other hand, even if we confine them to Irish novels, fall into both the literary and popular or commercial categories, with considerable overlap between the two. And within both broad categories are several sub-genres: post-modern, modern and classical realist, for instance, within the literary novel; chick lit, crime, thriller, romance and science fiction are just some of the genres of popular fiction. Arguably some of the latter can also be described as literary, as is certainly the case for science fiction, juvenile fiction and crime fiction.

The first challenge in teaching the novel is that as a genre it encompasses such a variety of forms. Creative Writing courses in the community acknowledge this to some extent. Inkwell, for instance, a commercial writing programme, offers workshops specializing in genres such as crime fiction, children's fiction, women's fiction, and so on.[6] But in the university, and in most of the community-based Creative Writing courses, 'the Novel', in its general unspecified form, is the subject *par preference*. To courses and modules on the novel come students with aspirations to write, or with manuscripts containing, all varieties of the genre: Old English sheepdogs and Great Irish Wolfhounds, pugs and poodles, fantasy, Gothic, mystery, science fiction, and – most

---

4 There are exceptions, notably in the form of 'flash fiction'. 5 Donald Barthelme, *Sixty stories* (London, 2003), p. ix. 6 See http//www.writerscentre.ie and http://www.writing.ie, accessed 10 January 2013. Inkwell offers courses on historical fiction, children's fiction, literary fiction, women's fiction and crime fiction.

frequently – the mongrel middle-brow literary novel, which by some Darwinian process has survived against the artistic odds. As David Lodge has noted in explaining this survival: 'post modernism it is widely believed, has consisted in ignoring, rather than in trying to go beyond, the experiments of modernism, reviving and perpetuating the mode of classic realism which Joyce, Woolf and Co. thought they had despatched for good'.[7]

The enormous plethora of guides to novel writing, like the courses, tend to pay scant attention to the varieties of the novel, and focus, by implication, on this mongrel. James Frey summarizes the situation:

> There are scores of books for the beginning fiction writer on the bookstore shelf, most of them helpful. A few of them, such as Lajos Egri's *The art of dramatic writing* (1946), Jack M. Bickman's, *Writing novels that sell* (1989), Raymond C. Knott's *The craft of fiction* (1977), Jean Z. Owen's *Professional fiction writing* (1974) and William Foster Harris's mighty little masterpiece, *The basic formulas of fiction* (1944), are extraordinary.
>
> And then of course there's James Frey's *How to write a damn good novel* (1987).[8]

While most guides purport, like that by Frey, to offer the key to writing 'a damn good novel', many focus more specifically on the market forces. Richard Webster and Brian Morris's title, *How to write a novel that becomes a bestseller*, would serve to describe dozens of books similarly promising the holy grail of publication, which is regarded, not unnaturally, as either success or as the first step on the road thereto.[9] This goal is also the carrot dangled by a batch of guides of a more negative hue, very like the dieting plans called '25 fattening foods you should never eat'.[10] Paula Berinstein, *42 common mistakes novelists make*,[11] is an example of a rash of handbooks which identify the 'carbs'

---

7 David Lodge, *After Bakhtin* (London, 1990), p. 25.   8 James Frey, *How to write a damn good novel, II: advanced techniques for dramatic storytelling* (New York, 1994), p. 1.   9 See, for example, K.M. Weiland, *Outlining your novel: map your way to success* (New York, 2011); Nigel Watts, *Write a novel – and get it publishd* (London, 2010); Jonathan Veale, *How to write a book or a novel: an insider's guide to getting published* (Kindle edition, 2012); George Green and Lizzy Kremer, *Writing a novel and getting published for dummies* (London, 2007).   10 See http// www.health.com/health/gallery: '25 fattening foods you should never eat', accessed 12 Jan. 2013.   11 Paula Berinstein, *42 common mistakes novelists make* (Kindle edition, 2012).

of fiction and offers recipes for achieving a slim, attractive novel which will win the race for readers, fame and money.[12] Another is the alarmingly entitled *How NOT to write a novel: 200 mistakes to avoid at all costs if you ever want to get published* by Howard Mittelmark and Sandra Newman.[13]

Creative writing programmes within the university offer both teacher and student the privilege, the time and the space, to read, write, think and learn in a nurturing environment, to forget about the pressures, fashions and absurdities of the marketplace, however temporarily, and focus on the art of writing for its own sake. Nevertheless, like the author of *42 common mistakes*, the teacher of the novel module is faced with the challenging task of dealing with a multi-faceted genre under a rubric or umbrella which seems to reduce the dozens of forms of the novel and the millions of individual novels to one entity.

There are a few strategies at this teacher's disposal. In the first place, even though the novel comes in so many forms, certain features are shared by the vast majority, if not by all, of them – for instance, language, voice, point of view, character, story and plot. Simply explaining these concepts, and providing illustrations of how they are applied in various novels, is useful, and probably the most common approach. Second, a teacher can, and should, define which kind of novel she is mainly dealing with, when employing that ambiguous word (meaning, after all, nothing more than 'new'). It is usually the mongrel: the classic realist literary novel. But whatever the idea of the novel that underpins the course and the teaching is, this needs to be clearly conveyed to students. They should be encouraged, or obliged, to read examples of that novel, and learn to read closely, analysing the way in which novels are composed. The type of novel at the heart of the module should ideally be the kind the teacher is writing or has written: experience of writing this genre is central to effective teaching. Nor should the focus of a module on a specific genre of novel discourage students from reading widely in many sub-genres and modes, or from writing what they need to write themselves. In an ideal creative writing programme, modules on science fiction, fantasy, crime writing and children's writing would be offered.

12 These are often treated as adverbs and adjectives.   13 Howard Mittelmark and Sandra Newman, *How NOT to write a novel: 200 mistakes to avoid at all costs if you want to get published* (London, 1966).

Simplification is a necessity imposed by the curriculum and the timetable. On the other hand, the restrictions of the novel module highlight some of the key issues of teaching in the contemporary university, and its very problems can be viewed as a virtue. Like the novel itself, the class on the novel is open-ended and polyphonic. Circumstances dictate that the workshop cannot be a closed system: the main work, of reading and writing, must be carried on outside its boundaries and must continue long after it finishes. The balance that has to be maintained between rules or guidelines and freedom and experimentation is supported, as it happens, by the very tensions produced by the impossibility of pinning down the novel in the classroom.

WRITING IN TIME

The abundant varieties of novel is one of the practical problems faced by teachers of modules focusing on theories of novel writing. For the facilitator of the traditional workshop devoted to novels, this may be less of a challenge, since workshops deal with the specific work in progress of students, and abstract theory arises only in connection with their work. Of course, in the size of class typical of an MA in Creative Writing – up to sixteen students – it is always the case that various sub-genres of novel are being written so a flexible approach to reviewing is required, on the part of facilitator and students.

Both taught module and classic workshop share the second major challenge the novel presents in the classroom, however. Even the most inclusive definitions of the novel, such as Jane Smiley's 'A novel is a (1) lengthy (2) written (3) prose (4) narrative with a (5) protagonist',[14] agree that a characteristic that is shared by all novels, no matter what their genre or quality, is that they are long. The issue of time is one with which every novel engages, inside and outside the parameters of the text. All narratives, oral, written, and even visual – films or graphic novels – exist mainly in time (whereas works of art such as paintings or statues, for instance, exist mainly in space). They always narrate an event or events which in its or their turn occurred in time – traditionally, in time past. Folktales, which include genres entirely fantastical,

---

14 Jane Smiley, *Thirteen ways of looking at the novel* (London, 2006), p. 14.

are almost always told in the past tense, seldom the present and never the future. No matter how unbelievable its content, the storyteller facilitates suspension of disbelief and compression of time by indicating that his tale happened: 'Once upon a time' or 'Long long ago'. A novel may present the story of an entire life, of eighty or ninety years, or several lives, within its limits of a hundred thousand words. In the traditional nineteenth-century novel, it was acceptable to present decades or centuries within the covers of a novel. The novelist developed devices to compress a hundred years into a limited number of pages, readable in eight to sixteen hours on average. In a novel, thanks to the novelist's skill in handling time, a reader can accompany a character through eighty years of her life in a space of ten hours, and in a gripping novel the reader readily suspends disbelief and feels she is present with the protagonist for the duration of the latter's story.

In tandem with the constraints imposed on perspective – the narrowing of the omniscient viewpoint to a single point of view – a narrower time frame has become more acceptable, if by no means standard, in the modern novel. James Joyce is, perhaps, one of the clearest examples of a Modernist writer; he presented a novel whose events occurred in the space of one day (most readers would actually take longer than a day to read the text). *Ulysses* is thus read in something closer to 'real time' than, say, *Middlemarch*, or *War and peace*, or *Little women* or *Pride and prejudice*. Twentieth- and twenty-first century novels deal with time in a variety of ways, some using the stratagems of the nineteenth-century novel, others locating the now of the novel in a very limited time frame – a day – and employing devices correlating to human memory to deal with time past. Ian MacEwan's *On Chesil beach* is a good example of the contemporary novel that observes unity of time and place. The top story is confined to one night and one location; the back story is expressed in flashbacks and summary of the future finishes a novel that deals with two lives from childhood to late middle age.

Novels have come up with various strategies to express time: the selection of significant events or scenes is the most common. Summary, compression and skipping over time are others. One of the many challenges for the novelist is to freeze the ever-flowing thing that is time, to trap it and pin it within the covers of a book. Like much that the novel tries to do, this is realistically impossible. Although time is a mysterious phenomenon, it is generally accepted philosophically and at the level of ordinary understanding as continually moving on. The shattered glass cannot go back onto the table and hold water. Except in stories and novels. The novel is, arguably, the shattered glass that has gone back up onto the table and is whole again. As D.H. Lawrence writes, in another context, 'Books are not life'.[15] But novels routinely succeed in pretending to be life, and in appearing to overcome the laws of physics.

For the reader it is easy to cope with the double standard regarding time that is essential to the novel. She can open a novel, left down a day or two days earlier, and quickly re-enter its time zone. Since last reading, the sun has set and risen, rain has fallen and dried up, grass has grown, meals have been cooked and eaten and dishes washed up. The reader has grown older. But when she opens the book she is immediately back in novel time.

The novelist, writing the novel, must attempt the same trick. She must manage time outside the text as well as within. It's harder for the writer than for the reader, though, because, when she opens her manuscript, on her computer or in her copy book or on her sheet of parchment, she has to write, in effect invent, the next page. Like the reader, she has experienced the sun setting and rising, the rain falling, the meals cooked and eaten, the delph washed. She too has changed and grown older since the day before, or the week before, and as a changed person comes to her next page and writes it. She has to find a way of freezing time, of pretending that today is yesterday or last year, of 'getting into' her own novel. That she succeeds, that all novelists succeed, in doing this, is testimony to the great twin powers of imagination and concentration. The novelist, working day by day and week by week and month by month, on a text that must eventually become a unified whole, imagines that time stands still while she is writing. Writers, describing the act of writing, often comment on this: 'I look up and five hours have passed'.

In books whose titles indicate that the problem of writing time is indeed viewed as highly significant, literary self-help gurus who rush to tell us how to succeed also offer tips to novelists on dealing with the problem of time, mostly expressed as ways to beat the tyranny of the clock. Louise Doughty, one of the more conservative members of this

15 D.H. Lawrence in Anthony Beale (ed.), *Selected literary criticism* (London, 1956), p. 105.

group, treats novel writing as long distance running and presents what looks like a reasonable training plan: *From first page to last in 52 weeks: a novel in a year.*[16] But according to Karen Wiesner and others, a novel can be produced in one twelfth of that time: *How to write a book in thirty days.*[17] Peter Kornfield twins the desirable goals of speedy efficiency and certain success in his *How to write a fiction book in thirty days that is sure to be a success.*[18] But Amy Bates piles on the pressure in *How to write your novel in ten days or less.*[19] Finally, for the Olympic sprinter novelist, Jack Marrow tells us *How to write a book in 48 hours.*[20]

There are examples of novels written at high intensity over a short period of time: John Boyne's *The boy in the striped pyjamas* was written over three days (and nights, without sleep).[21] Edna O'Brien wrote her classic *Girl with green eyes* in three weeks.[22] And many crime novels, children's novels, and chick lit novels may be written in a shorter time than the authors care to admit. But, although it is odious to generalize and great novels may be written at high speed – as the Edna O'Brien example indicates – in general a literary novel of sixty or seventy thousand words will take at least a year to complete, and much longer if the writer is occupied with a job, or with a Creative Writing programme which makes other demands on his time: classes, assignments, essays.

TEACHING IN TIME

Owing to the novel's length alone, it does not fit comfortably into the the Creative Writing workshop. This classic workshop, in which the student's writing is reviewed by teacher and peers, is closely related to the tutorial devoted to Practical Criticism, or New Criticism, the backbone of English literature courses in the period when the Creative Writing workshop began to flourish in the US – the 1950s onwards. Close reading, an intense focus on the words on the page, are common

---

16 Louise Doughty, *From first page to last in 52 weeks: a novel in a year* (London, 2008). 17 Karen Wiesner, *How to write a book in thirty days: a Guardian masterclass* (Kindle edition, 2012). 18 Peter Kornfield, *How to write a novel: how to write a book in thirty days that is sure to be a success* (Kindle, 2012). 19 Amy Bates, *How to write your novel in ten days or less* (Kindle edition, 2013). 20 Jack Marrow, *How to write a book in 48 hours* (Kindle edition, 2012). 21 Lecture delivered at Gotheborg Book Fair, September 2012. 22 Rachel Cook, 'Edna O'Brien', *The Observer*, Sunday, 6 February 2011, Review Section, p. 10. See http://www.guardian.co.uk/books/2011/feb/06/edna-obrien-Ireland-interview, accessed 12 January 2013.

to both. Practical Criticism works best with lyrical poetry, and following that, the short story – first, because both are metaphorical forms of writing, and second because both are short forms of writing. For Practical Criticism 'the short, artful prose narrative became ... second only to the lyric poem in its promise of reward for the sensitive reader ... More accessible than poetry, more manageable than novels, it was just the right size for a demonstration.'[23] Just as the lyric poem and short story suited the close reading of Practical Criticism, the short story suits the close reading that is also the main method of review in the Creative Writing workshop. There is enough time, in the workshop lasting two or three hours, to focus closely on the words on the page, since there are not so many pages to focus on. Most significantly, as well as critiquing images, lines, sentences, the short story workshop can also deal with the whole thing – the story with its plot, its arc, its meaning and its impact. The writer, whose work has been reviewed, will leave the workshop with the satisfaction of knowing that her short story in its entirety has been read and considered.

Owing to its length, the novel is never reviewed in a workshop in this way. Even if entire student novels are available – and usually they are not – students in a typical MA workshop are understandably reluctant to read and review up to fifteen novels (as are teachers). Perforce, the novel, whether in progress or in redraft, is considered piecemeal – its words, its lines and, at most, its individual sections or chapters are discussed and assessed in isolation from the whole. This is very useful and necessary, since all these aspects are essential components of the novel, and every novel is written in pieces and over time anyway. But every work of art is more than the sum of its parts, and the novel is no exception. David Lodge, commenting on the preference of literary theorists for metaphorical genres (such as the poem or short story), points out that the novel, by which he means the classic realist novel, is a 'narrative discourse, and narrative is a kind of language in itself that transcends the boundaries of natural language within which stylistic criticism operates most confidently and competently'.[24]

E.M. Forster is probably expressing the same idea in simpler terms when he says, in the oft-cited line, 'A novel tells a story'.[25] With a

23 See Susan Lohafer and Jo Ellyn Clarey (eds), *Short story theory at the crossroads* (Baton Rouge, 1989), pp 4–5.   24 David Lodge, *After Bakhtin*, p. 75.   25 E.M. Forster, *Aspects of the novel* (London, 2005), p. 25.

short story, or a lyric poem, the detail can be reviewed, but so can the total structure and the relationship of the parts to the whole, within the time alotted to the workshop. As readers, our experience of the short story or poem, while it is cradled in time, is closer to our experience of a painting, in that we can perceive the whole work at one go. This applies to the student's short story as well as to that of the established canonical writer. But whatever chance there is of dealing with the whole of a novel which is already written and published, well read and familiar to all the participants, in the timeframe of a seminar or a module, there is no chance of dealing with the work in progress of the student novelist. The student's novel is never considered as a whole in the workshop. Eventually, however, even though the time span for perceiving, that is reading, a novel is longer than the equivalent for a short story or a poem, the finished product will be absorbed in a very much shorter time span than that in which it was written (ten hours, Jane Smiley estimates, for the average 100,000 word novel).[26] It will finally be judged as a whole, not merely as the sum of its parts. Aesthetically, except for some kinds of metafictional novel, and arguably even there, the parts must cohere and in a very complex way.

So when one of my students, having finished her novel, commented – desperately – that she needs help with the structure of her novel, that the close editing is helpful but it's not enough, she has in fact discovered this essential difference between the novel and other genres of writing: that the whole narrative 'language' of the novel requires a different sort of review, at workshop level, from that which serves the lyric poem or even the short story. Lines, sentences, paragraphs and chapters have been workshopped. But the workshopee, trained in the Creative Writing programme, quite understandably feels abandoned when her whole novel is not reviewed in the same manner. She suspects that, even though all the component parts may be as good as she can make them, there may still be a major flaw with the work as a whole. And this suspicion is very well founded. In my experience as a writer, it is easy, when wrapped up in one's novel, to write chaotically and at great length – it is easier to go astray in a novel than in a short story. Once again, I presume this is related to length and time. While the energy of inspiration is often sufficient to send a short story into orbit, the novel requires constant rebooting. David Lodge observes that

26 Jane Smiley, *Thirteen ways of looking at the novel*, p. 15.

'writing a novel could be accurately described as a process of continual problem-solving or decision-making'.[27] But the problems may not be solved, and bad decisions or solutions to the continual process can create more and more problems. As Graeme Harper puts it, writing a novel is like travelling in outer space. On that long voyage in unknown territory it is easy to go astray.

THE IDEAL NOVEL EDUCATION

The neatly shaped feline short story finds a snug bed in the Creative Writing workshop, but the bounding barking dog that is the novel needs more time and space. When the university year is over, the would-be novelist usually discovers that she has still not written her novel, and is henceforward on her own. This may feel like abandonment to the student now accustomed to the company of fellow writers, to feedback, to a nurturing creative environment. But arguably it is a desirable outcome for a Creative Writing module. The graduate may need to feel the sharp edge of abandonment in order to become an independent writer.

At their very best, seminars, classes or workshops, on a Creative Writing programme, can only offer guidelines and advice to the students. The actual creative work, the learning to write, is always carried out in solitude and outside the classroom. Workshops provide some definite signposts and some suggestions, helping the novelist on his or her unique journey. But the travelling has to be carried out by the student, who is in command of the space craft.

The sense of incompleteness that the graduate of the Creative Writing novel course feels is, in fact, in full accord with desirable outcomes for graduates of Master's degrees, according to the National Framework of Qualifications, which outlines educational goals and policy for all levels of education in Ireland. One of the key competencies for Fourth Level or MA programmes described in the NFQ is that graduates should be 'self learners', and should have demonstrated knowledge 'that provides a basis for developing or applying ideas.'[28]

27 David Lodge, *The year of Henry James: the story of a novel* (London, 2006), p. 49.
28 *University awards and the national framework of qualifications (NFQ): Issues around the design of programmes and the use and assessment of learning outcomes* (FIN 2009). See http://www.nfq.ie/nfq/en/about_NFQ/about_the_NFQ.html, accessed 12 January 2013.

MA students should emerge with skills, aptitudes and the confidence to go on learning, developing and creating. The Master's programmes in Creative Writing in UCD and in other Irish universities demonstrably provide graduates with exactly the kind of skills required for an independent writing life. They learn the rudiments of literary theory. They learn to read closely and forensically, as writers. They become skilled reviewers of their own work and that of others. Writers must always be readers and learners, and the MA puts aspiring writers on the right road. Post-positivistic models of education emphasize the importance of 'uncertainty' and 'liminality' in training programmes.[29] Graduates should not feel that their learning experience is wrapped up and finished when they leave the university. The guidelines aspiring novelists receive in the course of the MA programme may well be exactly what is required.

Nevertheless, one can envisage a university programme that could satisfy the goal of uncertainty or liminality, while simultaneously offering more opportunity for development within the academy to the apprentice novelist – the level of support and guidance which is readily available to the short story writer or lyric poet, thanks to the structure of the Creative Writing programmes.

A perfect programme on novel writing would offer modules on theoretical aspects of novels, involving close reading of examples, in tandem with intense workshops devoted to novel writing, providing student novelists with the close guidance that they frequently desire. In the MA programme, which necessarily covers a broad range of genres, there is not time for both. UCD has dealt with the problem in its recently initiated MFA degree.[30] The MFA is a workshop-based programme, intended for students who have already completed an MA in Creative Writing. Class numbers are small – three is the maximum in each workshop situation. In the course of the academic year, students usually succeeed in writing a novel, or a collection of short stories. Their final submission for assessment is a 50,000 word piece of fiction. This is shorter than the average novel in English at the moment – half the length of Jane Smiley's average text, of 100,000

---

29 A.C. Ornstein and F.P. Hunkins, *Curriculum: foundations, principles and issues* (Boston, 2004), p. 213. 30 The Master of Fine Arts in Creative Writing was established in 2011 in University College Dublin.

words – but many contemporary novels are much shorter than that. Gradually over the year the students will read most of their respective novels, and, finally, the supervisor and examiner reads fifty thousand words, or most of the complete novel. But, significantly, not all.

This type of programme grapples with the challenge posed by the length of the novel and the timeframe in which it can be written, and would seem to be the type of academic structure that is best fitted to the 'teaching' of the genre. Arguably, however, a PhD programme would provide an even better model. Like the doctoral thesis, the novel is a lengthy and complex work, undertaken by a student who has already served a general apprenticeship to the craft and art of creative writing. The usual timeframe for a doctoral thesis – three years – is sufficient to accommodate comfortably the writing and revision of a complete novel, with an extensive self-reflective, exploratory but critical introduction.

There are many other issues of immense importance attaching to this topic of the novel and the academy. For instance, a doctorate in novel writing is clearly no guarantee that the novel will be published. But the criterion for awarding the doctorate, in cases of traditional PhD theses, is that the work is publishable, not that it will be published. Many other important questions arise as soon as the idea of PhD in Creative Writing is broached. For instance, what constitutes research? How can a novel be graded? Is there enough work involved in writing a novel to deserve the award of a doctorate? Indeed, all the basic questions regarding the suitablity of Creative Writing as an academic subject are raised, but even more emphatically as soon as a doctoral programme is under consideration. It is beyond the scope of this essay to discuss all of these interesting concerns. Many universities in the UK, and at least two in Ireland, have already dealt with the issues anyway, since they offer doctoral programmes in Creative Writing.[31]

It is feasible to argue, as I have above, that what a novelist needs is not the close supervision available in PhD programmes, but rather the more general foundation of the kind available in the Master's degree, a basis for embarking on the independent application of knowledge – in the case of the novelist, independently writing a novel. The life of an

---

31 Queen's University Belfast and NUI, Galway, both award doctoral degrees in Creative Writing.

artist is one of constant independent learning and independent practice. But this is true of every academic discipline and every field of learning. And, given that Creative Writing has established itself as a subject in Irish universities, as it has in the United States and in Great Britain, the logical consequence is that the great and most demanding form of literature, the novel, should find its home in the highest kind of academic degree programme. As D.H. Lawrence, who never, of course, took creative writing classes, and would have hated them, but who was a writer who reflected on process, and an excellent critic and literary analyst, wrote:

> The novel is the one bright book of life. Books are not life. They are only tremulations on the ether. But the novel as a tremulation can make the whole man alive tremble. Which is more than poetry, philosophy, science, or any other book-tremulation can do.[32]

If the university embraces Creative Writing, as it has done and must do, since Creative Writing is at the heart of the humanities and creativity is at the heart of every branch of research and learning, it needs to provide time and space for the writing and the development of the art of the most demanding and complex of literary forms, 'the bright book of life': the novel.

---

32 D.H. Lawrence, *Selected literary criticism*, p. 105.

Writing as process: truth and sincerity in the poetry workshop

MARY O'DONNELL

The Asian-American poet Li-Young Lee is quoted as saying: 'I heard a poet say to me, "Oh, I *hate* sincerity." And I thought, oh, what *do* you like? *Insincerity?* I don't get it.'[1] Mostly, people don't get it. Sincerity is perceived automatically as a good thing. But this is precisely what the American poet Louise Glück in her essay 'Against sincerity'[2] questions when she challenges the assumption that the word 'sincerity' is analogous to 'telling the truth'. As her argument and analysis of two sonnets by Keats and Milton suggest, absolute truth in the quotidian sense is *not* always interesting in terms of our writing. And in a workshop setting, it is sometimes problematic for participants when they discover that their truth – defined here as a literal re-telling of something that really happened – does not necessarily make for a good, strong, interesting or memorable work, whether we speak of poetry or fiction.

Some writers are addicted to 'sincerity' on the page. To encourage this, they make themselves available to every sensation, believing sensation itself is a resource whether it's bog-snorkelling, walking across the Gobi desert or ice-carving in Lapland – anything but deal with the frequencies of the ordinary self and experience. Over-exposure to sensation in the interests of accumulating feeling and reaction often lies behind an attachment to the idea of sincerity. The thinking is that if we write about the immediate and the personal, and expose it, this will sound exactly like honesty, and all poems are honest. But does it? And are they?

I have often facilitated workshops in which someone writes a poem that describes a harrowing event that actually occurred – a death, an abuse, a loss, a hurt. Sometimes the person weeps because the reading

---

1 'Li-Young Lee on Poetry', 14 June 2007. See http://www.robertpeake.com, accessed 10 December 2012. 2 Louise Glück, 'Against sincerity', *American Poetry Review*, 22:5 (1993), 27–9.

unpicks that raw and damaged part of their being and now resurrects the pain associated with it in public. Often, people are swayed by this emotion, and conclude that the emotion that has caught the writer in its maw has helped to create an outstanding poem. The creator, the poet, is herself upset, so this must mean she has really engaged with something important. That may be, but great emotion on its own does not make great art. And in a workshop setting there is a fine line between being aware of the writer's feelings and mood, but also at some point, whether through general discussion or in a one-to-one conversation, encouraging her/him to take a step back from the emotion, and look again at the poem.

The writer wants the poem to be authentic. By authentic, I mean that it needs to have the flexion and torsion that allow a reader who does not know them, from any country, to read it and experience a sense that this poet is using the tools of language and emotion to establish a truth or raise a question about something that possibly lies *beyond* language and emotion. Louise Glück remarks that 'truth on the page need not have been lived, but envisioned.'[3] It is this envisioning that interests me as a teacher of writing, and the risks taken in order to separate the autobiographical self from a self of a different order, which inhabits a space behind the autobiography, and may possess a more compelling truth at its heart that is not strictly emotional.

Honest speech is a relief and not a discovery. When we speak of honesty in relation to poems, we often mean the degree to which the initial impulse has been transcribed. But what about transformation? Any attempt to evaluate the honesty of a text must always lead away from it, and toward intention. This may make an interesting trail, more interesting, very possibly, than the poem. The mistake, in any case, is our failure to separate poetry that sounds like honest speech from honest *poetic* speech.

Part of my task, when in a workshop, is to encourage apprentice writers to value the words 'artistic' and 'creation', because a real acceptance of those two words precedes any work they undertake and is something that can't be over-valued. They are two of the components of a tripartite concept that can sometimes help writers discover an authentic voice. The third component is process, which demands

---

3 Louise Glück, 'Against sincerity', p. 28.

patience and the cultivation of an inner artistic calm. This sense of calm is necessarily linked to a cerebral ability to detach from the initial urgency (if the writing has been triggered by an urgency) or indeed the initial stumbling approach, and to question the self that has written down a first draft, to take a step back and simply wait.

Creating the habit of patience in a writer takes time. There are impediments that interfere with that process. For example, artistic work today occupies the dubious position of being over-valued for its celebrity status, but under-valued on the level of the home office, the production room or the imagination, the result being that occasionally an impatient writer arrives into a workshop looking for lists of outlets, publishers and agents – straight away. There is a tendency among some beginning writers to regard it as a hobby option – something to be slotted in after work, or between school runs. While I accept (from experience) that indeed writing for some people (especially women) is often unavoidably grafted on to the tail end of daily obligations, it is not the ideal way to proceed and it is worth emphasizing to all apprentice writers that this is not a part-time occupation, nor do one or two drafts mean that a work is finished. One of the most important goals of any module is to convince the participants that they must re-draft, then view from a distance, and re-draft again, as often as necessary until the poem, or fiction, is polished and perfect. The art, in a sense, is in the willingness to craft; the inspiration in the motivation to step back and cultivate coolness and to balance this with emotional truth.

Other impediments may be the tendency for some beginning writers to consider canonical poetry as inhibiting or elitist, usually when cultural references they are not familiar with are embedded in a work. Before anything happens in a workshop regarding nailing down what we mean by truth when we write, other issues must be addressed. For example, some people are moved to write a kind of protest-poetry. They find themselves agitated by such things as litter, smoking, unmarried mothers, tax evasion, young people pushing and shoving, young people drinking or generally anything to do with young people, and cruelty to animals. They take on these subjects and present a world view through their poetry that attempts to force everybody else to see life as they do. But is this what poets do, I ask? Is that the essence of our work? While subjects themselves are not generally the problem, the manner and tone of their making might well be. It is not the case that poets and fiction writers do not judge, because surely every word they write is imbued with personal vision, response and attitude. But real writers address the question of tone, which seems vitally important if one is to avoid a work that amounts to a high judgment on the human race and its frailties. Consequently, the question of writing something that isn't trying to convert the world emerges and with it how to advance a writer's work towards a realization that might address these subjects in some way, but with a less judgmental approach.

Accepting the truism that writing happens out of silence, it must be recognized that when participants enter a workshop they often carry the baggage of the outer world – with accrued perceptions of what to do, how to go about it, and what other people will say. They come with expectations, ambition, feeling and some anxiety. Before anything is written, it can be useful to discuss these concerns. As their teacher, I am naturally curious about the participants' reading habits, if any. It is striking that for too many, a vital connection has not been made between reading and writing and that if one habitually does the former, it will become a significant influence on the outcome of the latter.

A major concern based on personal observation and exchanges with participants is the fact that while the majority of women in a literary workshop (by which I mean, one which has selected a group of serious beginning writers) are frequently aware of what is being published in their area of interest, and are regular readers of literature, middle-aged and older men are not reading with any particular urgency and do not appear to view it as something necessary to their writing experience, especially if the authors are female. The gender of the author influences the decisions men make about what to read. While women do not appear to have a gender bias in their reading, only younger men share the same literary habits, and read, regardless of gender. This raises an interesting question for me as a teacher of writing: if a few men are presenting themselves in a writing workshop or module, who have not read fiction written by women, does this suggest a lack of curiosity about human experience in general. Curiosity and intellectual inquisitiveness pursued through reading often complement a real writer's life and this is something I tell them. It is also worth remarking that I am aware of female participants in some groups who have opted to do a Creative Writing option because yoga or French were full up. It is equally difficult to work with them. As a writing teacher, I am largely interested in participants who wish to become writers.

People often ask if creative writing can be taught. Any reply to this is necessarily qualified. Experience suggests it cannot be taught at all, but that statement may be coloured by my encounters with the male writer who refuses to read work by women because he does not believe he has anything to learn from female perception and the female writer who is too busy with the multitude of things that busy women engage their time with to concentrate exclusively on making artistic work beyond pastime level.

But I benefited from several Creative Writing workshops when I was starting out. The encouragement of the poet John F. Deane, who led a workshop I attended in Listowel, Co. Kerry, in 1982, with regard to an unfinished poem of mine led me to believe that my ideas about writing poetry were ones I could perhaps put into practice. His enthusiasm generated self-belief in me. I returned from Kerry in a state of high excitement and set to the task, producing about twenty new poems in the ensuing two weeks – most of them scrawny efforts, all legs and neck, but one or two of which were fair attempts that made their way into print. I also subscribe to the theory that, with the right encouragement and some technical assistance, someone with writing talent can undoubtedly come closer to being the writer they want to be through a writers' workshop, or a university-based writing module.[4] The worst outcome is that they will become better readers and marginally better self-critics (and it is no harm to have better readers, given that many are untutored in deciphering, for example, a novel and its characters. I am speaking of people who read novel after novel, do not recall any of the titles, and confidently 'hate' unsympathetic or complex characters because they are not pleasant).

Inherently, I am always scouting for the apprentice writer who may already be a writer and not quite realize it. Or for the person who recognizes that language contains dynamite properties to which only

---

[4] It may not be what the mentor wants them to be, of course, and therein lies another interesting psychological knot for Creative Writing teachers: the fostering of a mutual awareness that teachers and writers (of talent) may tread a solid path together for a time, before the inevitable fracture that is healthy for apprentice writers. The latter must go their own way, perhaps discard what the teacher has 'taught', in order to realize their own vision, and ultimately split from an influential mentor.

his or her emotional energies can be the imaginative catalyst. But, on a technical level, how does one approach the work of writing poetry? Many years ago, I participated in an event, advertised as a women's poetry workshop that aimed to focus on technique. In the end, it meant that the facilitator brought her stringent and observant eye to bear on the collective offerings of our group that included what were to become several of today's well-known poets of my generation. There were many present, and as with large numbers everywhere, a one-day workshop cannot adequately approach the question of technique. Nonetheless, for those of us interested in a life in writing, the day event was encouraging. There was a coming together, a questioning, a day-long gesture made in favour of the imagination.

Early on in poetry workshops I usually raise the issue of end-rhyme and invite those, who have never written anything else but end-rhyme, to break the habit for a few weeks, because I want participants to acquire a new one – perhaps that of freely putting words down, and working with words that are sometimes based on prompts. I want them to feel free to play, in an experimental sense; I want students who are extremely well-versed in the vocabulary of poetry analysis, to break for a while from that pattern so that they can re-consider and relax about received signals considered integral to poetry. This is not to discount the value of being aware of the language of critical analysis in literature, but initially for me, a concern to see words on the page is uppermost. Once that happens, we are, as a group, in a position to engage with the process of writing, and to ask several things, among them:

- What is the truth or essence of this poem (or story)?
- Are the words as the writer has laid them down, 'earning' their space on the line (page)?
- Are the words pushing towards a truthful revelation?
- Are they doing what the writer intended, but also (significantly), what she did not? In other words, is the writer gearing up through her imagination to allow words to emerge which were perhaps unplanned, and yet in the end seem necessary?
- We can also enquire as to whether what the writer thinks may be the truth is actually denying the emergence of a more artistically apposite truth.

But before all that, further preparation is necessary. As a facilitator, I need to know that the word *image* is understood: what this can mean, how it has been used by other poets and what is its underlying intention. I also need to have discussed some notions of musicality and rhythm with reference to canonical poems but also to many not belonging to a fixed canon. I believe in discussing the traditions out of which poetry has emerged, historically, in order to demonstrate that it is a constantly evolving, shifting linguistic force. It is important to provide examples of a variety of poems through photocopies or a powerpoint presentation so that students test these ideas through the texts provided.

One of the most liberating things for a writer to recognize is the encounter with *sound* itself. It is vital to demonstrate through a sample text – especially for apprentice writers who favour end-rhyme (often doggerel) – how often rhyming sound occurs at different points within a poem. Once students become aware of assonantal sound, for example, or consonantal echoes, either mid-line, or at the end of one line and the beginning of another, it can free them to catch the essential balance between being 'loose' and 'concentrated', between wanting to say something specific, and allowing themselves to add to it in ways they had not anticipated because end-rhyme was so emotionally confining. It is easy to identify in any group the poets who are already engaging with process. They are often the ones who make it up, who do not stick to prompts because they have acted as a non-literal catalyst that sends them off on a unique trajectory.

How often do I deploy what is usually referred to as a 'prompt'? Occasionally. Experience teaches that the apprentice who is frozen in the act of attempting to write just might gain access to a beginning through the use of a prompt. This can take several forms. Some writers respond readily to certain words, whether monosyllabic or multisyllabic. Others respond to concepts or to the prompt of the seasons of the year. Groups of words that suggest elemental aspects of the natural world are useful to yet other writers, such as earth, air, fire and water. Others can build on these by reimagining colours that, for them, may connect with elemental images. Such a process does not necessarily result in the writing of a strong poem. What it does, frequently, is to get an apprentice writer beyond the halting, inhibited stage, in which every word is questioned and negatively judged even as she or he has begun to create or shape the work.

During weekend workshops, I try to set a small amount of time aside for music. Either the writers listen to this and do nothing else, or they are free to write down notes or ideas that occur to them. It sometimes takes time for a group to transfer from the hectic world of obligation, to a world that thrives on quiet, and where there are no obligations other than to do your best. While the music is playing, my hope is that the writers' sense of time may expand, and that there are no anxieties regarding failure or incompleteness. What I want eventually to achieve is the release of a flow of writing, a torrent of words which can later be examined by the group. It is important to maintain a controlled but unthreatening dynamic as one wants to draw responses from the group which may offer assistance or validation to the writer. It is not a question of sharing work for therapeutic purposes, so much as exhibiting it in order for others to participate in the action of the work that is offered.

Depending on the education and attitudes of a group, I have sometimes attempted to apply the Socratic method because I believe that humans are intuitively aware of much more than we realize. In such a case, if the probes and questions are correct, a writer will deduce what he or she might write that will improve the work, without my declaring 'this is right, this is wrong, you should do it this way'.

Experience also confirms that some writers come to a workshop with preconceptions about what is about to occur and about the outcome of the workshop. A professional woman who once attended my poetry workshop did so because she hoped it would improve her ability to translate a French text she was working on. On another occasion, someone presented me with lines for a poem that were written diagonally in a frail, illegible scrawl on a page of foolscap. Because I have the experience of knowing someone who lives with brain injury, I mistakenly assumed her writing was that of one whose co-ordination had been damaged. I was wrong. When I questioned her she informed me that she had decided to write with her left hand in order to see if it released her creativity.

Conjointly, the facilitator herself needs to tread with care and carefully examine her own baggage. If students present themselves to a group with accrued assumptions formed by various self-oriented life coaching or other therapies they have attended, it is my duty to advise them that writing involves a different kind of process: it demands an ability to free the self from mannerisms and emotional frigidity, because ultimately we write in search of an unstated truth.

The facilitator also needs to be quite clear as to what her expectations are. It is not my role to demolish someone's work, to mock, undermine or ridicule. I mention this because I know that it occurs, if rarely. However, it is my role to encourage the participant to begin to write, and having achieved that end, to then lean in closer to examine a range of available techniques. I tell students not to shy away from the question of influence. We are all influenced by others but an individual style eventually emerges from beneath the mantle of influence, especially if the writer continues to read often and carefully. Reading is the other vital aspect of the Creative Writing module or workshop. It is like a lining on the stomach that allows all new and freshly experimented-with writing 'foods', to rest on, to be turned over by, to be digested and absorbed and generally strengthen the writerly 'body'.

Participants who are already readers of contemporary poetry and fiction strike me as being less concerned with the self in an autobiographical sense, although what they invent may indeed paradoxically be inspired by their response to experience. Hanif Kureishi has contended that experience is all we have to write about.[5] We can't go shopping for it. We can't buy it. We simply have it, no matter who we are or where we come from; we must recognize that this is all we have.

But, as Louise Glück notes, we sometimes confuse experience with sincerity, believing that sincerity equals poetic truth. It does not. The interrogation of experience can only come through process. Such re-examination invites the writer to look on a work as slowly evolving, to be prepared to wait it out even when uncertain about goals. Writing, then walking away, and later returning to re-view are a necessary part of the process of creation. Rushed work comes from the pressure to be a celebrity, to be what is called respectfully a well-known writer. But most well-known writers are never heard of again after their own lifetime and people in workshops should be made aware of this clarifying piece of information.

Quite a number of contemporary Irish writers have participated in workshops themselves, finding it necessary and welcome in their early careers to come to a greater awareness of what they wanted to do and

5 Hanif Kureishi, *Dreaming and scheming: collected prose, reflections on writing and politics* (London, 2002).

achieve. Most of the women of my generation who went on to publish have taken part in workshops as apprentices, possibly more than the men. During the 1980s the workshop had a slightly subversive quality in that it was seen as an unthreatening environment in which a beginning female writer could broach her work. But it had its critics too, many of them highly suspicious of what actually happened within these groups. To this day, the majority of participants in workshops are female. The question of why this is so may be the subject for another essay. But some decades ago women in Ireland simply did not feel confident enough about the business of writing as a life vocation, about calling themselves 'writers', about setting out on that journey unaccompanied, or indeed about testing out the subjects they wanted to treat. It is only in retrospect that I as a writer realize how repressive my own culture once was for its creative women.

Today, workshops are not gender-specific in the same way. In them, men and women can successfully learn how to lose the dross and how to pull back from the edge of indulgent writing; they can learn, through craft and practice, how to carry on and be resolute. Through the discovery of re-drafting and of patience, through the elimination of the pedantic inner judge, they can discover how to read better. Most importantly, in the end, they can learn how to accept that only through process, which invites a different level of honesty than that which ordinarily documents our living, can art turn into authentic creation.

What we talk about when we talk about talking: writing dialogue in the novel and short story

JAMES RYAN

The large array of literature modules on offer in third-level colleges testifies to the great variety of ways in which the novel and short story can be encountered. A novel can, for instance, be considered in terms of thematic elements, its place in the canon, the ideological positions espoused or rejected and so forth. However illuminating these perspectives may be, they are not of direct value in the development of the craft of fiction writing, unless, of course, they specifically set out to analyse the process of composition. This process is of the greatest interest here. Coming to understand it entails looking at the component parts of a novel or short story and investigating how they work and interact.

The approach outlined below is based on a view of the novel and the short story as first and foremost, works of the imagination for the imagination. Consequently, factors which inhibit, compromise or in some way detract from an imaginative response feature to a considerable extent. Before considering these factors it is necessary to look at the main literary forms for which dialogue is written. These include screen, stage, radio, the novel and short story. While the process of creating dialogue for each of these forms is similar, it is not the same. It is worth investigating what makes them different, emphasizing the manner in which an audience engages with each. If, for instance, an audience is provided with a visual setting as in stage drama, then the dialogue is necessarily different from that which might typically appear in a novel. Consequently, awareness of the potential audience must be given due consideration. It is a central tenet in discussion about the craft of writing creatively and particularly in the writing of dialogue.

After some of the differences between writing dialogue for stage drama and fiction have been identified, the ways in which dialogue is signalled in the novel and the short story can be brought into focus. These include inverted commas, indentation, line spacing and dashes.

Students might consider whether each of these forms of denotation makes the same imaginative demands on a reader. The objective in posing this question is to demonstrate that the form of dialogue denotation a writer selects is based on the extent of the imaginative challenge he or she wishes to present to a reader. If none of the conventional modes of denotation are used, the imaginative challenge is considerable. This point was made by Peter Cunningham in a review of Thomas Keneally's *The people's train:*

> There is a problem, however. Keneally has chosen to dispense entirely with conventional forms of presentation in regard to dialogue. Whereas most writers present dialogue between inverted commas, and some introduce dialogue with a hyphen, Keneally has removed all such conventions in this novel. The result is a challenge to the reader.[1]

When conventional forms of denotation are removed, the writer must find other ways not just of signalling dialogue but of indicating who is speaking. Syntax and language registers are among the most obvious ways of identifying speakers, but this calls for considerable skill. Even with such skill, there is always the risk of confusion. The corollary, of course, is predictability: dialogue which can be anticipated in advance. Puzzlement is part of the reading process. It is a criterion by which fiction is frequently judged. Hilary Mantel, for example, notes, in reference to Susan Hill's novel, *The Beacon,* 'the author is clever enough to leave our minds humming with doubt'.[2] Striking the balance between puzzlement and predictability is *the* age-old problem facing writers. This problem emerges at all stages in the composition of a novel, character construction, plot, pacing and for present purposes, dialogue.

The imaginative pitch of a novel or short story takes the imaginative reach of audience into consideration. The imaginative reach of a five-year-old, for instance, is not the same as that of a twelve- or an eighteen-year-old. The notion that different age groups, and perhaps different genders, generally seek different forms of imaginative engagement is an important one. It opens the way to understanding that a work

1 See Peter Cunningham, 'Book of the day', *Irish Times,* 18 October 2009.   2 Hilary Mantel, 'Author, author', *Guardian,* 23 January 2010.

of fiction is composed within certain imaginative parameters and, crucially, that these parameters play an important part in shaping many elements of the work: length, language register, range of reference and dialogue.

Dialogue, like so many other elements of a novel or short story, serves many functions. It is widely used both in the construction of character and in defining, or creating an impression of, relations between characters. It can be a means through which information or misinformation is conveyed. It can conjure setting. Difficulties arise, however, when it is put to too many uses at the same time. Take for instance, the use of dialogue in constructing a character. Here, individual speech patterns and language registers come into play. If on top of that an author, seeking to advance the narrative, gives such a character great swathes of raw information to reveal, then the value of dialogue in constructing that character will be diminished. This is one of many conflicts that arises in the process of composition. Some of these can be resolved by deciding, in advance, or indeed in the process of writing itself, what part, first and foremost, a particular piece of dialogue is to serve. Is it to convey information? Is it to create a sense of place? Is it to vary the narrative pattern? It may do all of these things, but is more likely to work well both in itself and in the novel as a whole if a writer concentrates on one above the others. Arguably, the objective that should take precedence for the student of Creative Writing is character. If in the course of dialogue a character becomes less convincing because the author has decided to convey a series of facts that that character is unlikely to know, then a revision is called for. Equally, if a character is loaded down with background data, then he or she may become a mere cypher. Either such data is seamlessly incorporated into the dialogue, which will almost always entail reducing the amount of information divulged, or another way of conveying it is found.

Asked, in a seminar on dialogue, to write a short piece illustrating a character weighed down by background detail, one particular student seized the opportunity to dramatize the point amusingly:

> 'Don't mention Bray.' Said John defensively. 'That was where I was going when I heard my best friend Tim was killed in a car accident on his honeymoon in Chile, which straight away

reminded me of the other car crash that happened two years ago next month, the one where all my family were killed on the way to my wedding where I got married to Samantha who I broke up with six weeks ago when I met you.'

'That's right, it is six weeks ago since we met on the seafront. It was the day after I lost my job, the day when ...'

Any authenticity this exchange might have had is undermined by the extent to which the characters are employed to provide the back story.

Authenticity can be achieved in many ways, not least through incoherence. Identifying circumstances where muddied dialogue might be effectively used is very worthwhile. For instance, are certain emotional states sometimes best conveyed through incoherence? One of the objectives in raising this question is to break down established patterns of sentence construction and to explore, appropriate to context, the potential of fragmented language, non sequiturs, repetition and misuse.

Dialogue written in the form of a pit-pat volley format can reduce the impact of a work. It relegates the readers to the status of observer or listener, depriving them of the pleasure of configuring, puzzling over and speculating on the exchange. There are no hard and fast rules here, just some pitfalls to be avoided. The most obvious of these is the straightforward wholly coherent question/answer sequencing, repeated over a number of pages. This becomes even less acceptable when the questions and answers are of similar length. A piece of dialogue may, in the process of writing, start off like that. And for many writers it does, but only as a prelude, through editing and revising, to making that dialogue both engaging and authentic.

Attribution plays a significant part in the imaginative challenge presented by dialogue. This can be illustrated by analysing a piece of fiction in which there is sustained dialogue, directing students to note patterns of attribution, in particular, the extent to which the dialogue is tagged, *John said / Mary said*. This creates a context in which students can consider whether persistent tagging supports or undermines an imaginative response.

Very skilled practitioners, working in what might be broadly termed realism, tend to minimize the use of tagging. The opening section of John McGahern's *The Dark* provides an apt illustration.[3] A close examination of this, focusing on attribution, will reveal how little McGahern relies on the use of 'said' to indicate who is speaking. The passage has been constructed to ensure that the reader can immediately identify each of the two speakers. Developing a piece of fiction to this stage is likely to require a great deal of work.

Discussion of the lack of reliance on attribution in this section of *The Dark* can be brought a step further by asking how McGahern has ensured that the reader can immediately identify who is speaking. There are many elements for consideration here. Chief among them is the extent to which the characters in the dialogue are defined. They are sharply contrasting on a range of grounds: power, physical strength and temperament. The corollary points to the difficulties thrown up by characters in a dialogue who are not well defined or who are very similar.

The capacity to negotiate the many different concerns that emerge in the writing of a novel is crucial, not so much in the beginning stages as in the ongoing editing process. This is where balance between the various elements is most likely to be achieved. Analysing archival material that displays work in progress, as referred to above, is very worthwhile for learning how skilled writers strike that balance between conflicting concerns.

When it does become necessary to attribute dialogue with the verb 'said', then a writer must decide where it can be best positioned. If relentlessly placed directly after what has been said, then it can become monotonous and may result in a lack of engagement. Placing it within what is being said, as McGahern does, makes it less conspicuous:

> ... 'I'll teach you a lesson for once', he said with horrible measured passion through his teeth, the blood mounted to his face. 'I'll teach you a lesson this house won't forget in a hurry.'[4]

In general, varying where 'said' is placed will reduce the disruptive potential of frequently repeated use. Varying the attribution verb may

---

3 See John McGahern, 'Undated draft of *The Dark*', *The John McGahern yearbook*, 3 (2010), 36. The manuscript of *The Dark* is available in the McGahern archive in NUI Galway where many of his manuscripts are held. See http://archives.library.nuigalway.ie/mcgahern/.   4 John McGahern, *The Dark* (London 1960), p. 9.

have the same impact, but it presents other problems. It can draw unwanted attention to attribution, so much so that many contemporary writers avoid such usages. Illustrating this point, John Mullan, for example, picks up on the wide range of attribution verbs in chapter six of D.H. Lawrence's *Women in love*:

> ... one finds the words of the characters being 'protested', 'cried', 'exclaimed', 'retorted', 'whispered', 'asseverated', 'stated', 'asked', 'persisted', 'commanded', 'jeered', 'replied rather superbly', 'said in contempt', 'said warningly' and 'squealed.'[5]

Making dialogue more engaging calls, not for variety in the range of attribution verbs as exemplified above, but for variety in other methods of signification. If, for instance, a character follows speech with a gesture, or addresses – by name – the person to whom she or he is speaking then a reader is presented with an imaginative task, which albeit minor, is frequently preferable to the flat, factual note struck by 'said'. This verb can, of course, serve many purposes as well as attribution. Its extensive use, as in Roddy Doyle's, *The Snapper*, for example, is only partly to alert a reader to who is speaking.[6] Its greater function here is to catch something of the story-telling style of the characters who people this novel. As such its frequent use, or purposeful overuse as the case may be, plays an important part in the narrative, serving to create and uphold authenticity, to locate the action and build the characters.

Exchanges involving several people compound the difficulties posed by attribution. Different ways of alerting a reader to who is speaking may be of use to a writer in trying to do this, but equally may make for awkward narration. Contemporary writers, who consider attribution as intrusive, may well decide that it does not matter who is speaking. Their primary concern is with the cut and thrust, or equally with the seamless flow, of a series of exchanges in a group. Consequently, attribution is sacrificed to this enterprise. In Colum McCann's *Let the great world spin*, the need for attribution is largely dispensed with in the pivotal scene in the novel, a tight rope walk between the twin towers, by having an initially unidentified witness to

5 John Mullan, *How novels work* (Oxford, 2006), pp 135–6. 6 Roddy Doyle, *The Snapper* (London, 1990).

this event describe what is going on to a lightly sketched California-based computer hacker named Compton. This is one of a number of cryptic exchanges, some of which are peripheral to the event, presented in rapid succession in this scene:

> – I told you so, shouts Compton.
> – Who's this? says the voice.
> – Far out!
> – Who the hell is this?
> – Is he still on the tightrope?
> – What's going on? Are you messing with me, man?
> – Is he still there?
> – He's been up there twenty, twenty-five minutes!
> – All right! Is he walking?
> – He is going to kill himself.
> – Is he walking?
> – No, he's stopped right now!
> – Standing there?
> – Yeah!
> – Yeah, he's got the bar going. Up and down in his hands.
> – In the middle of the wire?
> – Near the edge.
> – How near?
> – Not too near. Near enough.
> – Like what? Five yards? Ten yards? Is he steady?
> – Steady as shit! Who wants to know? What's your name?[7]

McCann's objective is first and foremost to present the event in as immediate and startling a way as possible. To develop the characters commenting on it would be to diminish its import as would the repeated use of an attribution verb. Speech is signalled by dashes and there are no adverbs, accelerating the pace and so adding further urgency.

The use of an adverb, indicating how something is said, is a practice which, in recent years, has come in for debate as in the following observations by Elmore Leonard:

---

7 Colum McCann, *Let the great world spin* (London, 2009), p. 179.

> 'Never use an adverb to modify the verb "said"' ... he admonished gravely. To use an adverb in this way (or almost in any way) is a mortal sin. The writer is now exposing himself in earnest, using a word that distracts and can interrupt the rhythm of the exchange.[8]

It would appear that this warning, supported as it is by other practitioners, is based on the belief that a reader ought to be given the opportunity to imagine, rather than be told, how something is said. This forces a more considered approach to the writing of dialogue. The writer must find a way within the actual wording of a piece of dialogue, to convey the manner in which it is expressed.

A simple seminar exercise can be used to get this notion across to students by presenting them with a piece of dialogue as follows: 'Close the door', she said crossly. Students are asked to rewrite this, omitting the adverb, while retaining the way in which 'Close the door' is said. There are many possibilities for reworking the sentence, depending on the character of the speaker: 'Would it be too much trouble to close the door after you?' Or 'Shut the bloody door.' And so forth. Students might then be asked to identify the words, phrases and syntax in the above exchanges, which eliminate the use of the adverb 'crossly'. Considering dialogue with this criterion in mind is an effective way of editing to good effect.

Adverbs in dialogue, however frowned upon, have many important parts to play and should not be completely ruled out, despite Elmore Leonard's strictures. If, for instance, a writer wishes to locate a piece of fiction in the historic past, then the conventions of composition used in the period in question may help to create a sense of that past. This is exemplified in Alan Hollinghurst's *The stranger's child*.[9] This novel spans the twentieth century, honing in on five specific eras. The success with which the early periods in the century are evoked is based to a considerable extent on the use of conventions of composition associated with those periods, featuring, appropriately, adverbs in speech attribution. This strategic use gives the prose what might be termed an antique character. Furthermore, Hollinghurst's particular choice of adverbs both establishes and reinforces the authenticity of the privi-

8 Elmore Leonard, Interview, Review Section, *Guardian*, 20 October 2010. 9 Alan Hollinghurst, *The stranger's child* (London, 2010).

leged strata of British society featured in the novel. Seminar exercises can be devised to experiment with this, but are unlikely to be of use to the majority of those interested in the mechanics of composition. Making the point is sufficient. Less complex and more familiar to students is the widespread use of adverbs in children's or teen fiction. Indeed, many authors in these genres take the opposite line to that advocated by Elmore Leonard. The maxim would seem to be: always use an adverb. And with good reason. Children and many readers of teen fiction respond imaginatively to adverbs linked to speech attribution. Consider, for instance, the following: 'Let's go to the island', said John excitedly.

'Excitedly' is not perceived by a child as an instruction on how to interpret the way in which John spoke, but rather as an imaginative proposition in itself. J.K. Rowling in the *Harry Potter* series offers considerable scope to illustrate and explore this point.

Insights into attribution can be gleaned from a study of dialogue at any point in the evolution of the canon. Creative Writing courses devised to parallel a student's experience in embracing works widely held to be of particular significance in that canon might, for instance, go right back to the Anglo-Saxon period. In some of the earliest secular texts, 'The Battle of Maldon' (a narrative poem about a battle between the English and the Vikings in 992), great effort is taken to ensure that there is no confusion about who is speaking. The following excerpt contains no less than three verbs, 'called out', 'spoke out' and 'declared':

> þa stod on stæðe, stiðlice clypode
> wicinga ar, wordum mælde,
> se on beot abead brimliþendra
> ærænde to þam eorle, þær he on ofre stod.
>
> [There stood a Viking messenger on the shore;
> he called out fiercely, spoke out in [these] words,
> declared in threat the sailors' message to the nobleman, where he stood on the bank].[10]

---

10 See 'The Battle of Maldon: Hypertext Edition', http://www.english.ox.ac.uk/oecoursepack/Maldon.

The need to ensure that there is no confusion about who is speaking here can be examined, using a short class exercise along the following lines: First, establish the context in which this narrative poem was written. Then, consider the nature of the audience for whom it was composed, keeping in mind literacy levels and oral traditions. To what extent do these factors determine the way in which speech is attributed? The objective here is to impress on students how an awareness of audience can determine the nature and extent of attribution. This, in turn, might be related back to children's fiction.

Students of Creative Writing, taking a craft and composition course, of which the above is one component, present a portfolio at the end of the semester containing a short assignment on each of eight or nine components. One reasonably effective form of assessment for such a class on dialogue is an assignment in which students are presented with a photograph of two characters and asked to write a piece of dialogue of around 500 words, without providing any ancillary narrative. The stated aim in writing this piece of dialogue is to take into account some of the issues raised in the class. Equally, students might be presented with a piece of dialogue from a short story or novel and asked to consider it critically, using some of the criteria raised in the course of the class.

In this discussion of the writing of dialogue, presented as a contribution to the discourse on the teaching of Creative Writing, some of the factors shaping the form dialogue takes in the novel and short story were considered. Particular attention was paid throughout to both audience awareness and the need to ensure that dialogue engages a reader imaginatively. Factors perceived to inhibit such engagement, such as an over-reliance on dialogue to provide back story, lack of care in attribution and the rash use of adverbs, were reviewed. These, in turn, were offered as criteria of potential value to the editing process, but not universally so. Dialogue, it was observed, serves may different functions in the composition of novels and short stories. Editing is necessarily guided by a variety of concerns and a work of fiction is best served by a capacity to negotiate these concerns effectively.

Grading creativity

MARY MORRISSY

'Everywhere I go, I'm asked if I think universities stifle writers. My opinion is that they don't stifle enough of them', Flannery O'Connor.

It was a university in the southern states of the US. I was teaching my first workshop on an MFA in Creative Writing programme – my first workshop, ever, actually. It had been a steep learning curve. For me, that is. As a self-taught writer, I had only attended one writers' workshop as a participant – they were not part of the culture of 1970s Ireland. As a teacher, I was learning from my students the jargon for skills I had been using instinctively for years – motivation, back story, point-of-view. When they talked about the Iowa model, I wondered if it was a car, or a catwalk they were discussing, whereas it was the template for workshop practice established by the Iowa Writers' Workshop in the US.

At the end of term, I gave one student a C grade for a story she had submitted as part of her final assessment. When she got the result, she sent me a barrage of recriminatory e-mails. Did I realize what this meant? This would bring her grade point average down. She was an MFA student and Master's students simply didn't get Cs. Mistakenly, I tried to reason with her. I stopped when she wrote back in large capitals: LADY, WHAT WERE YOU ON WHEN YOU GRADED THIS? There were further threats suggesting that she knew where I lived and that she and her boyfriend might come round to visit. I might have treated this lightly, but several years previously, a post-graduate student in the same English department, enraged by poor grades, had shot dead a professor before turning the gun on himself. Grading in this context, I realized, was a matter of life and death.

For the past twelve years I have earned the major part of my living from teaching Creative Writing, both in Ireland and the US. I have taught both inside and outside academe – in community workshops and writing groups on the one hand, and at undergraduate and post-graduate level in universities, on the other. The biggest difference between these two strands of teaching experience is grading.

Engaging with adult writers in a community setting is, for me, the 'purest' form of Creative Writing teaching, precisely because there is no marking. The community workshop is primarily about inspiring creativity. Technique and craft come into it, of course, but at beginners' level especially, it's about instilling confidence, kick-starting the creative process and guiding the new writer towards the spring of the sub-conscious. To paraphrase Flannery O'Connor, it's about encouraging the 'habit of writing'.

There are huge rewards for the teacher in the community setting. Witnessing a student finding her voice, or seeing a tyro writer getting to the end of a piece of writing, can be deeply satisfying. But these breakthroughs may be short-lived; there is no guarantee that the spark you've ignited in class will extend beyond it. People come to writing classes for a myriad of different reasons that have nothing to do with acquiring literary expertise or going on to a life in writing. Nevertheless, the spirit of creative collaboration that flourishes in community workshops does so because the teacher is free to mentor and the student is free from the threat of judgment.

Much the same atmosphere pertains to teaching Creative Writing at undergraduate level in Ireland. Writers-in-residence, appointed on a visiting basis, will often lead undergraduate writing workshops but these generally operate outside the curriculum and do not entail assessment. In fact, the creative writer in the Irish university can often feel like an outsider, the part-timer who sneaks in after hours offering a craft workshop like a teacher of macramé or a pottery instructor.

In the US, however, Creative Writing at undergraduate level is sewn into the system and is, therefore, graded. Marking at this level is less daunting – and dangerous – than at post-graduate level. The reason for this lies in the more liberal approach to third-level education in the US. For many of the undergraduates in the American system, Creative Writing is at worst, an easy option, or at best, an elective, experimental choice. The students come from all faculties, not just English; this semester they might be taking Creative Writing, next they might be studying microbiology or fashion photography.

Like their community workshop counterparts, they are, essentially, amateurs. (I don't mean this as a disparagement. After all, in formation, I am an amateur writer.) But for the most part, Creative Writing undergraduates are experimenting, playing with the notion of writing, trying it on for size. This very playfulness can produce some lovely work. I am often amazed at pieces that young students have produced in class at short notice in response to a prompt. There is often a quick-silvery brilliance to such writing, though it is, by its nature, a hit-and-miss affair. Students often don't know how they achieved interesting effects, and they mightn't necessarily be able to reproduce them. But the delight in teaching at this level is that students – perhaps out of ignorance or innocence – will take writing risks because, paradoxically, they are less invested than the post-graduate writer.

In such classes, of course, there is a huge range of abilities and varying degrees of seriousness and ambition. When it comes to grading undergraduate writing, I find that I'm assessing basic competence – the ability to shape short pieces of writing – and the engagement with the creative process. I am marking on the sincerity of the attempt rather than a polished end product.

Which brings us to grading at MFA level. Here is where the heartaches begin for the Creative Writing teacher. Why is it *so* different? Well, firstly, there is a vocational component in a Master's level course. Now the student is exercising career choice, opting for specialization and focused ambition. The MFA student is generally older and no longer 'playing' at writing. As a teacher, I believe you have to treat MFA students as if each and every one of them is going out into the world to be a writer, although this is not necessarily the case. One of the downsides of the Creative Writing industry in US universities is that, more often than not, you are training students not necessarily to be writers, but to be teachers of Creative Writing. In his broadside against the MFA system, Avis Shivani noted that before the 1950s, the ideal for the literary writer was 'to be free of the restraint the academy, or really any institution, imposes'. Now, literary writers not attached to the academy 'are almost nonexistent'.[1] On the other hand, in today's harsh publishing climate, the university is often the only sanctuary for the literary writer, where her work will be supported, read and appreciated.

1 A. Shivani, 'The MFA/creative writing system is a closed, undemocratic, medieval guild system that represses good writing', *Boulevard*, 26 (2010), 26

But such patronage comes at a price and that price is grading. Teaching at MFA level does not involve different skills. The same encouragement of students, the creation of an atmosphere of trust and patient shepherding of talent is required. But now you must start to impose professional strictures. Students are expected to have a conscious awareness of craft, a degree of technical know-how, a sense of sustained application, an appreciation of deadlines. Ideally, the MFA course should engender an atmosphere of creative hothousing. But the measuring of creative work, which the university system requires, demands from the teacher the very opposite of those nurturing qualities she draws on for teaching. Assigning a letter grade is the antithesis of a qualitative response to work and undermines the constructive criticism that is the hallmark of good literary mentoring.

The structure of MFA programmes is such that, for most of the time, the teacher is a hand-holder. You set up a supportive but critically robust workshop environment that allows students to learn from their peers and their peers' work. The workshop should develop the students' writing skills and enhance their critical faculties, so that they can self-edit their work when they no longer have the support of their collegiate community of writers. I always tell MFA students to savour this time. Never again in their working lives as writers will they enjoy such concentrated attention; they have several faculty members at their disposal, whose sole job it is to consider and reflect on their work. What luxury! In these hard times, no editor or agent will have the time or the inclination to mentor their writing in this way.

But come the end of the MFA programme, the teacher has to switch hats. Now you're no longer the caring mentor but the dispassionate judge delivering a verdict. This requires a particularly violent *volte-face*. For the student, it can be a disturbing sensation to find a supportive professor turn overnight into a mean marking machine. The sympathetic educator must now rate that most sensitive of concepts – the student's sense of self as expressed on the page. (All writers will tell you that this is why rejection hurts; it is *always* deeply personal.) For the teacher, her fledgling writers are lined up firing-squad style to be evaluated in competition with one another. The academic system demands not only measurement, but a uniform mode of evaluation of creative work, even though no two pieces can be said to be alike. How do you compare one novel with another? Or how do you decide that *this* novel is better than *that* volume of short stories?

In assessing creative work, you are faced with a host of questions, less to do with the work under review than with your role. Who do you represent when you grade? Are you standing in for the outside world of publishing – an interesting position for a writer to be in, impersonating the very people she herself is trying to impress. Are you like the commissioning editor picking up a manuscript from the slush pile? Isn't that terribly subjective? Well, yes, but isn't that what all writers face – subjective reactions from editors, reviewers and readers? Are you judging student work on its saleability in the world outside the academy? Or are you looking at a piece of writing as you would a Master's thesis in English literature? Do you grade for improvement, or promise? Do you take into account contribution to class? Does a writer have to do a lot of talking in class to score highly? Is that relevant to a career in writing? Are you measuring outcome or effort? Welcome to the world of systemized creativity.

Even after twelve years, I don't really know how I grade Creative Writing. I only know that the quality of the writing must come first. That means, inevitably, rewarding raw talent, which, paradoxically, the student arrives with; that is one thing you can't teach. I try, when evaluating student work, to acknowledge and then ignore my own prejudices. After all, I wouldn't be much of a writer, let alone a teacher, if I couldn't admire and appreciate writing that I mightn't choose to read. In the end, though, there's always the fear that I'm simply marking out of a gut instinct.

Whatever criteria the Creative Writing teacher uses to measure her students by, it must appear very unscientific, and by academic standards, fatally lacking in rigour. As Mark McGurl asserts, Creative Writing in the university context is 'an experiment – but more accurately – an exercise – in subjectivity.'[2] As in all faculties, grade inflation has crept in. Kelcey Parker, an MFA graduate herself and now a Creative Writing professor, remarks, that there is 'a culture of, if not quite A-for-effort, A-for-playing-nicely. If you show up, slog through the steps of the writing process, have something chipper to say about

---

2 M. McGurl, *The program era: postwar fiction and the rise of creative writing* (Cambridge, MA, 2009), p. 405.

your classmates' writing, and turn in a final draft that's different from the first draft, congratulations, you get an A.'[3]

But what all these doubts and misgivings lead to is the question no-one wants to ask, least of all the shoals of financially challenged writers like me who earn their bread from teaching – does Creative Writing belong in the university? Is that the real contradiction in terms? And if the academy insists on measuring creative activity, does it, in the end, have the courage of its own convictions? In all my years of teaching, I've never heard of a student failing an MFA. Is it possible to do so, I wonder? What would you have to do to get an F? Never to attend? Produce porn? Shoot your teacher, perhaps?

---

3 Quoted in K. Parker, 'The myth of subjectivity', *talking writing*, 5 September 2011. See http://www.talkingwriting.com, accessed 10 December 2012.

Contributors and editors

GERALD DAWE is the author of seven collections of poetry, most recently, *Points West* (2008). His *Selected poems* was published in 2012. His other publications include *The proper word*, a volume of collected criticism, the memoir, *My mother-city*, *The world as province: selected prose, 1980–2008* and *Conversations: poets & poetry*. He has also edited several anthologies of Irish poetry and criticism. A fellow of Trinity College Dublin, he is professor of English, and founder director of the Oscar Wilde Centre for Irish Writing at Trinity College Dublin.

RODDY DOYLE is the author of nine novels, a collection of stories, and *Rory & Ita*, a memoir of his parents. He won the Booker Prize in 1993, for *Paddy Clarke ha ha ha*. He has written for the stage and his plays include *Brownbread* and *Guess who's coming for the dinner*. He also wrote the screenplays for *The Snapper*, *The Van*, *Family*, and *When Brendan met Trudy* and co-wrote the screenplay for *The Commitments*. He lives and works in Dublin.

CARLO GÉBLER was born in Dublin in 1954 and is a writer. He has taught creative writing at Queen's University Belfast and the Oscar Wilde Centre for Irish Writing, Trinity College Dublin. He is currently writer-in-residence in HMP Maghaberry, Co. Antrim. He lives outside Enniskillen, Co. Fermanagh, Northern Ireland, and is the author of several novels, non-fiction works, plays, scripts and articles.

SINÉAD MORRISSEY is the author of five poetry collections: *There was fire in Vancouver* (1996), *Between here and there* (2002), *The state of the prisons* (2005), *Through the square window* (2009) and *Parallax* (2013), all published by Carcanet Press. Her awards include the Patrick Kavanagh Award, the Rupert and Eithne Strong Award and the Michael Hartnett Poetry Prize. In 2007 she received a Lannan Literary Fellowship and her poem 'Through the Square Window' was awarded first prize in the UK National Poetry Competition.

MARY MORRISSY is a novelist and short story writer and has published three novels, *Mother of pearl* (1995), *The pretender* (2000), *The rising of Bella Casey* (2013), as well as a collection of short stories, *A lazy eye* (1993). She won a Hennessy Award for short fiction in 1984 and a

Lannan Literary Foundation Award in 1995 (sharing the honour that year with Alice Munro and Louis de Bernieres). *Mother of pearl* was shortlisted for the Whitbread Award (now Costa) and *The pretender* was nominated for the Dublin IMPAC Award and shortlisted for the Kerry Group Irish Fiction Award. She currently teaches fiction on the MA in Creative Writing at University College Cork.

MARY O'DONNELL's collections of poetry include *The place of miracles: new and selected poems* (2006) and *The ark builders*. The Hungarian edition of her poems has recently been awarded the Jelen Könyvek Translation Prize. Her fourth novel, *Where they lie*, is forthcoming from New Island in April 2014. Her seventh collection of poetry will also appear from Arc Publications UK in 2014. She teaches poetry and fiction on NUI Maynooth's creative writing programme, and is a previous judge of the Dublin IMPAC Literary Prize, the Hennessy Literary Awards, the Strokestown International Poetry Competition and the Irish Times Poetry Now Competition. She is a member of Aosdána. She received the President's Alumni Award at NUI Maynooth in 2011.

NESSA O'MAHONY lives in Dublin, where she works as a freelance teacher and editor. She is an associate lecturer with the Open University, and also teaches at Oscail, the Dublin City University distance learning programme. She was writer in residence at the John Hume Institute for Global Irish Studies, University College Dublin, 2008–9. She has a Masters in Creative Writing from the University of East Anglia, and a PhD in Creative and Critical Writing from Bangor University. She has published three volumes of poetry; a fourth is forthcoming from Salmon Poetry.

LEANNE O'SULLIVAN comes from the Beara peninsula in West Cork and received an MA in English from University College Cork in 2006. The winner of several of Ireland's poetry competitions in her early twenties (including the Seacat, Davoren Hanna and RTÉ Rattlebag Poetry Slam), she has published three collections, all from Bloodaxe, *Waiting for my clothes* (2004), *Cailleach: the hag of Beara* (2009), winner of the Rooney Prize for Irish Literature in 2010, and *The mining road* (2013). She was given the Ireland Chair of Poetry Bursary Award in 2009 and the Lawrence O'Shaughnessy Award for Irish Poetry in 2011 and received a UCC Alumni Award in 2012.

PAUL PERRY is author of three poetry collections, *The drowning of the saints* (2003), *The orchid keeper* (2006) and *The last falcon and small ordinance* (2012), which Dermot Bolger described as 'the work of a singular imagination', and of a collaborative novel, *Goldsmith's ghost*. A winner of the Hennessy New Irish Writer of the Year Award, he is Curator of the Dún Laoghaire–Rathdown Poetry Now International Festival and teaches Creative Writing at Kingston University, London and University College Dublin.

JAMES RYAN grew up in Co. Laois. He has written four novels: *Home from England* (1995), *Dismantling Mr Doyle* (1997), *Seeds of doubt* (2001) and *South of the border* (2008). He is director of the Creative Writing programme at the School of English, Drama and Film, University College Dublin. The focus of his postgraduate research, M.Ed., was the development of creativity in the context of formal education.

EDITORS

ANNE FOGARTY is professor of James Joyce Studies at University College Dublin. She is co-editor with Luca Crispi of the *Dublin James Joyce Journal*.

ÉILÍS NÍ DHUIBHNE is a novelist and short story writer. She has published more than twenty books. She teaches creative writing at University College Dublin. Her latest collection of short stories is *The shelter of neighbours* (2012).

EIBHEAR WALSHE is a senior lecturer in the School of English at University College Cork. He is the author of *Kate O'Brien: a writing life* (2006) and *Cissie's abattoir* (2009).

Index

Ackerley, J.R. 74–6; *Hindoo holiday* 75; *My dog Tulip* 75–6
Akhmatova, Anna 52
Alcott, Louisa May 107; *Little women* 107
Allen, I. and J. Seaman, *Going the distance: online education in the United States, 2011* 81
Amnesty Ireland 41
Anderson, Linda 83; with Derek Neale (ed.) and Bill Greenwell, *Advanced Creative Writing* 83
Arlen House 14
Armitage, Simon 52
Arts Council of Ireland 24–5; 'Writers-in-Prisons' scheme 25; 'Writers-in-Schools' scheme 25; Irish Writer Fellowship (with Trinity College Dublin) 25 n 6
Arts Council of Northern Ireland 25; 'Writers-in-Prisons' scheme 25; 'Writers-in-Schools' scheme 25
Associated Writing Programs 64
Association of Writers and Writing Programs (AWP) 16 n 20
Attic Press 14
Austen, Jane 107; *Pride and prejudice* 107
autobiography 21, 93–100, 117, 124

Bachelard, Gaston 64
Bangor, University of, Great Writing Conference 16 n 20
Barrett, Colin 15
Barthelme, Donald 103
Bates, Amy 109
Batuman, Elif 30–1
Beck, Heather 85, 91
Belfast 11, 53, 78

Beowulf 60
Berinstein, Paula 104–5
Bickman, Jack M. 104; *Writing novels that sell* 104
biography 22, 96
Bishop, Elizabeth 28
Blasket Island writers 77
Boland, Eavan 55–6
Bowen, Elizabeth 98–9; *Seven winters* 98
Boyne, John 15, 109; *The boy in the striped pyjamas* 109

Carpenter, Andrew 10, 15
Carson, Ciaran 52
Carver, Raymond 9–10
Cassill, R.V. (Associated Writing Programs) 64
Cavafy, Constantine 52
Chekhov, Anton 75, 103
chick lit 103, 109
children's writing 105, 109; *see also* fiction
classical realism 103
community workshops 14, 29, 136–8
concrete poetry *see* poetry
Cooke, Emma 12 n 13
Creative Writing 19–21, 25, 28–30, 33, 46, 63, 69, 82, 140–1; accreditation 25–6; American prototype of teaching 10; as a concept 26; as a subject 22–3; as an academic discipline 10, 14, 22, 101, 114, 140; at NUI Maynooth 10, 10 n 6; at Open University in Ireland (OU) 82–7, 89–92; at Queen's University Belfast 10; at Trinity College Dublin 10, 14, 25; at University College Cork 10; University College Dublin 10, 14–15, 102; courses 9, 11, 23, 26,

82–3, 112, 134; 'Creative Writing corporation of America' 64; degree in 9, 20, 23, 25–6, 101; community-based courses 103; de-institutionalization of 64; in an online environment 81–92; in Australia 10; in Ireland 9–10, 15–16, 18–19, 20, 22, 24–34, 101, 115, 136–7; in the community 16, 103; in the UK 10, 15, 115; in US 10, 19, 29–30, 102, 115, 136, 138; Iowa Writer's Workshop 9–10; Master's level 10, 15, 17–18, 91, 106, 112–14, 136, 138, 140; MFA 15, 17, 64, 113, 136, 138–40; networks 26; non-academic courses in Cork, Dublin, Galway 25–6; pedagogy 18–19, 63–4; PhD in 53, 114; poetry module 46–7; programmes 11, 15, 19–22, 29–30, 63–4, 101–2, 105, 115; residential weekends 26; teachers/teaching 16–17, 20–1, 28, 55–63, 137, 140; teaching of in Irish universities 10, 27; techniques 82; tutors 66, 69; undergraduate modules 10, 52, 82, 137; word association experiment sample sheet 70; workshops 10–12, 14, 17, 20, 23, 25, 55–7, 63–70, 93–100, 109–10; see also Open University in Ireland; Queen's University Belfast; Trinity College Dublin; University College Cork; University College Dublin; University of Stockholm

crime fiction 103, 105, 109; see also fiction
critical writing 20, 24, 87–9, 96, 121
Cross, Michelle 64
Cunningham, Peter 127

Damasio, Antonio 67
Dawe, Gerald 9–11, 20
Dawson, Paul 63
Deevy, Teresa 11

Dickens, Charles 32
Dillon, Éilís 24
Doughty, Louise 108–9
Doyle, Roddy 15, 20, 37–8, 131; *A greyhound of a girl* 37–8; *A star called Henry* 37, Henry Smart 37; *The Commitments* 37; *The Snapper* 37, 131
drama 28, 94–5, 97, 100; dramatic writing 82, 86; stage 126; television 11 n 11
Dublin 35, 41, 58–9; see also Creative Writing
Duchamp, Marcel, 48
Duffy, Carol Ann 50, 52
Dunn, Nell 74–6; *Up the junction* 74

Eggers, Dave 40
Egri, Lajos 104; *The art of dramatic writing* 104
Ekphrasis 47, 51
Eliot, George 107
Engle, Paul 9
English: departments 63, 136; departments in Ireland 19–20; faculties 137; language 31–2, 45, 76, 113–14; literature classes/courses 76, 109; literature, Master's thesis in 140; subject 16–17, 76; syllabus 13 n 16
Enright, Anne 15
Epic of Gilgamesh 60

Farley, Paul 48, 50; 'Relic' 48, 50
fantasy 103–5
Faulkner, William 9
fiction 17, 28, 30, 42–3, 71–80, 82, 93–5, 97–101, 103–4, 111, 113, 116, 118, 124, 126–30, 133, 135; American fiction 19; children's fiction 103, 103 n 6, 134–5; crime fiction 103; 'flash fiction' 103 n 4; teen fiction 103, 134; popular fiction 103; science fiction 103–5; women's fiction 103, 119

Index

Fighting Words, Dublin 25–6, 35–6, 38–41;
folk-tales 12, 103, 106
Forster, E.M. 110
Fortnight 78–9
Foster Harris, William 104; *The basic formulas of fiction* 104
Foster, R.F. 11
found poem *see* poetry
Frazier, Adrian 10
Freud, Sigmund 66–7, 69
Frey, James 104
Frost, Robert 55

Galway 24; *see also* Creative Writing
Gébler, Carlo 21; 77–80; *Driving through Cuba* (1988) 77–8; *The glass curtain* (1991) 77–8; *Father & I* (2000) 79–80; *Confessions of a catastrophist* (2013) 79–80
genre writing 33
Gillis, Alan 51
Glück, Louise 116–17, 124; 'Against sincerity' 116
graphic novel 106
Greenwell, Bill 83; with Derek Neale (ed.) and Linda Anderson, *Advanced Creative Writing* 83
Guth, Sarah 92
Gwynn, R.S. 51–2; 'Mr Heaney' 51–2

Hardy, Thomas 52
Harmon, Maurice 10 n 2
Harper, Graeme 101
Harte, Jack 14
Heaney, Seamus 52, 55–6
Hemingway, Ernest 68
Hill, Susan 127; *The Beacon* 127
Hillmann, Brenda 67
Hollinghurst, Alan 133–4; *The stranger's child* 133–4
Hosbaum, Philip 11, 25 n 5

'How can it be taught?: Teaching and learning Creative Writing in Ireland', Royal Irish Academy, Academy House, Dublin 16
Hunt, Celia 65

Illinois, University of, Center for Online Learning, Research and Service 82
imitation poem *see* poetry
Inkwell (commercial writing programme) 103, 103 n 6
Iowa Writers' Workshop (first MA in Creative Writing) 9–10, 18, 102, 136 *see also* Creative Writing
Ireland 13–16, 18–19, 26–8, 45, 57, 97; in the 1970s 12–13, 22, 136; in the 1980s 22; contemporary writers in 19–20; Fourth Level competencies 112; MA programmes 112; poetic tradition in 60; third-level education in 19–20; transformation from oral culture 13; universities in 114; university education and literature in 19; *see also* Creative Writing
Irish 51; academic world 28; academy 9; language, writers in 15 n 18; literature 19–20; memoir/s 96–8; novels 103; programmes 18; rural communities 13; short story 103; society 25–6; state policy 25; teaching practices 18; universities 10–11, 14–17, 22, 25, 82; writers and writing 12, 14–15, 17, 19–20, 24, 96, 124
Irish Press, 'New Irish Writing' page 14
Irish Women Writers' Club 11
Irish Writer Fellowship *see* Trinity College Dublin *and* Arts Council of Ireland
Irish Writers' Centre, Parnell Square 14

Jacob, Rosamond 11
Jarrell, Richard 45

Joyce, James 19, 103–4, 107; *A portrait of the artist as a young man* 19; *Ulysses* 107
Jung 66–8; 'The Association Method' 68

Keane, John B. 12 n 12
Keegan, Claire 15
Keneally, Thomas 127; *The people's train* 127
Kennelly, Brendan 25
Kiely, Benedict 12
Kilroy, Claire 15
Kilroy, Thomas 10, 24–5, 31–2
Kindles (e-readers) 33
Kleinzahler, August 64
Knott, Raymond C. 104; *The craft of fiction* 104
Kornfield, Peter 109
Kureishi, Hanif 63, 124

Larkin, Philip 51–2; 'Mr Bleaney' 51–2; 'This be the Verse' 52
Lavin, Mary 12
Lawrence, D.H. 108, 115, 131; *Women in love* 131
Lee, Laurie 77; *Cider with Rosie* 77
Lee, Li-Young 116
Leonard, Elmore 132–4
life writing 21, 71–80, 82, 94–6, 100
Listowel Writers' Week 12, 12 n 12, 14, 120
Lodge, David 104, 110, 112
London Review of Books 30
Longley, Michael 52, 55–6, 59; 'Once' 59
Love, Seán 41
Lynch, Patricia 11

Macardle, Dorothy 11
MacEwan, Ian 107; *On Chesil beach* 107
MacMahon, Bryan 12, 12 n 12

Macquarie University, Australia 91
Madden, Deirdre 15
Mahon, Derek 25 n 6
Maldon, Battle of 134
Manchester Metropolitan University 85; MA course in novel writing 85
Mantel, Hilary 127
Marcus, David 14
Marrow, Jack 109
Martin, Augustine, *Exploring English I* 13 n 16
Mason, Patrick 24
Maupassant, Guy de 75
McCann, Colum 131–2; *Let the great world spin* 131
McCarthy, Thomas 57, 59–60
McGahern, John 24, 93–4, 129–30, 130 n 3, *The Dark* 129–30, 130 n 3; 'The Man in the Moon's autobiography' 93–100
McGurl, Mark 15, 19, 30–1, 140; *The program era: postwar fiction and the role of Creative Writing* 30–1
Meehan, Paula 55–6
memoir 80, 93–100
Menand, Louis 30–1; 'Show and tell: should Creative Writing be taught?' 30
MFA *see* Creative Writing
Mittelmark, Howard 105
modernism 22, 32, 103–4, 107
Molloy Carpenter, Dorothy 14–15
Moodle (course management system) 82–4; Moodle-tools 89
Morris, Brian 104
Morrissey, Sinéad 21, 22
Morrissy, Mary 12, 16–18, 21
Mullan, John 131
Murray, Paul 30
Myers, D.G. 63

National Women's Writers Workshops 14
National Writers' Workshop 11, 15, 24

Index

Neale, Derek (ed.) 83; with Bill Greenwell and Linda Anderson, *Advanced Creative Writing* 83
New Criticism *see* Practical Criticism
New Yorker 30
Newman, Sandra 105
Ní Dhuibhne, Éilís 21
non-fiction 28, 76–8
North America *see* Creative Writing
Northern poets *see* Queen's University Belfast
novel 13, 19, 21, 24, 27, 30, 32–3, 37, 43, 46, 75–7, 84–5, 93–4, 100–15, 120, 126–35, 140; 'Campus Novel' 18–19; children's novel/s 109; chick lit novel/s 109; classical realist novel/s 110; crime novel/s 109; novel workshop 101–15
NUI Galway (MA in Writing) 10, 15
NUI Maynooth *see* Creative Writing

O'Brien, Edna 109; *Girl with green eyes* 109
O'Brien, Flann 19; *At swim-two-birds* 19
O'Brien, Kate 94–100; *Presentation parlour* 94–5, 98, 100
O'Connell, Jamie 15
O'Connor, Flannery 9–10, 136–7
O'Connor, Frank 12, 68
O'Donnell, Mary 22
Ó Faoláin, Sean 12, 98; *Vive moi* 98
O'Mahony, Nessa 21
O'Sullivan, Leanne 22
O'Sullivan, Maurice 77; *Twenty years-a-growing* 77
O'Tuairisc, Eoghan 24
Odyssey, The 58; Odysseus 58
Open University in Ireland (OU) 82–3, 85–6, 90–1; framework 90; Level Two 82; Level Three 82; teachers/tutors 84–5, 92; A174 Start Writing Fiction 86; A215 Creative Writing 82; A363 Advanced Creative Writing 82–4, 86, 89–90; End of Module Assignment (EMA) 83, 89–90; Virtual Learning Environments (VLEs) 82–3; *see also* Creative Writing
Owen, Jean Z. 104

Padel, Ruth 46; *52 ways of looking at a poem* 46
Parker, Kelcey 140
Patterson, Glenn 15
Perry, Paul 16 n 20, 18, 20; *Beyond the workshop* 16 n 20
Phillips, Adam 66–7
poetry/poetics 13–15, 21, 25 n 5, 26–8, 27–8 n 9, 32, 45–63, 65–7, 69, 82, 94, 97, 100, 110–11, 115–25, 134–5; concrete poetry 47; found poem 47–51; imitation poem 47, 50–2; lyric poetry 49, 110–11, 113; poetry workshop 27, 56, 60–2, 116–25
Poet's House 25
Poetry Ireland workshops 11
Poolbeg Press 14
post-modernism 14, 103–4
Practical Criticism 109–10
Proust, Marcel 98

Queen's University Belfast 10; 'Group' of Northern poets 11, 25 n 5; MA in Creative Writing 10; PhD in Creative Writing 10; *see also* Creative Writing

Rich, Adrienne 45
Robinson, Elizabeth 67
romance 103
Rooney, Wayne 36
Rowling, J.K., *Harry Potter* series 134
RTÉ radio 98

Salkeld, Blanaid 11
Sampson, Fiona 65

San Francisco 40–1; Center for Psychoanalysis 67
Sartre, Jean-Paul 75
Scham, Wilbur 9
Seaman, J. and I. Allen, *Going the distance: online education in the United States, 2011* 81
sestina 47
Sheehy Skeffington, Hanna 11
Shivani, Avis 138
short story 13–14, 36–7, 95, 102–3, 110–13, 126–35, 140; workshop 12 n 13, 110
Simpson, Louis 27–9, 27–8 n 9, 32
Smiley, Jane 9–10, 106, 111, 113–14
sonnets 47, 58, 116
Stairs, Susan 15
Staples, Heidi Lynn 65
Stephens, James 73
Stockholm, University of, Department of English, MA programme 10
Stone, Ruth 55–6
Swift, Patrick 93

Thoreau, Henry David 12
Thornfield Poets 14–15
thriller 103
Tichborne, Chidiock 59
Tolstoy, Leo 107; *War and peace* 107
Trinity College Dublin: MPhil/Masters programme in Creative Writing 10, 14, 25; Irish Writer Fellowship (with Arts Council of Ireland) 25 n 6; School of English 25 n 6; Writer Fellow, Oscar Wilde Centre 14, 30; *see also* Creative Writing
Tynan, Katherine 11

United Kingdom 16, 19, 45; publishers based in 26; universities 25, 82, 114; *see also* Creative Writing
United States of America (US/USA) 9, 12 n 12, 15, 16, 16 n 20, 19, 27, 27–8 n 9, 40, 45, 72, 109; in the 1960s 136; students 81; third-level education 137; universities 136; *see also* Creative Writing
University College Cork, MA in Creative Writing 10; *see also* Creative Writing
University College Dublin (UCD) 13 n 17, 14–15; Anglo-Irish literature and drama at 10 n 2; Department of English 10 n 3; graduate programmes in Creative Writing 102; unaccredited writing workshops 10; *see also* Creative Writing
University College Galway 11, 24

villanelle 47, 52

Walshe, Eibhear 21
Webster, Richard 104
Wiesner, Karen 109
Wilde, Oscar 95–8; *De profundis* 98
Wilde, Oscar, Centre *see* Trinity College Dublin
Wilmot, Seamus 12, 12 n 12
Wolfhound Press 14
Woolf, Virginia 99, 104
writing workshops 12, 12 n 12, 14, 17–18, 20, 22, 26, 29–31, 53–62, 101–15, 136
Wyndham, Frances 76

Yeats, W.B. 11–12